# Reading the Runes

# Reading the Runes

*A Beginner's Guide*

Kim Farnell

Zambezi Publishing Ltd

Published in the UK: 2003, 2005
by Zambezi Publishing Ltd
P.O. Box 221 Plymouth,
Devon PL2 2YJ (UK)
email: info@zampub.com
www.zampub.com

British Library Cataloguing in Publication Data:
A catalogue record for this book
is available from the British Library

ISBN 1-903065-26-7

# Contents

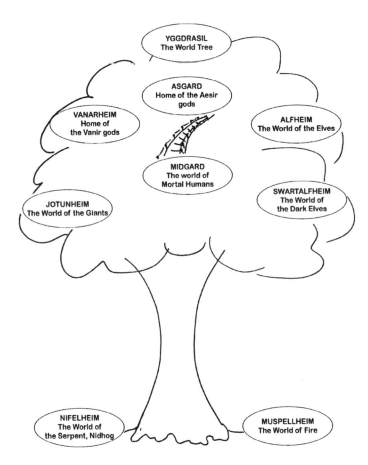

YGGDRASIL
The World Tree

ASGARD
Home of the Aesir
gods

VANARHEIM
Home of
the Vanir gods

ALFHEIM
The World of the Elves

MIDGARD
The world of
Mortal Humans

SWARTALFHEIM
The World of
the Dark Elves

JOTUNHEIM
The World of the Giants

NIFELHEIM
The World of
the Serpent, Nidhog

MUSPELLHEIM
The World of Fire

# The Nine Worlds

# What are Runes?

*Know how to cut them, know how to read them
Know how to stain them, know how to prove them
Know how to evoke them, know how to score them
Know how to send them, know how to spend them.*
FROM THE BOOK OF THE HAVAMAL

Runes are letters of an alphabet that developed from extremely ancient illustrations, each of which once had a specific meaning. These gradually developed into an ancient form of writing, which can be traced back from markings that appeared on rocks as early as the Neolithic period. Among the signs engraved on these early Runes were parts of the body, weapons, animals and variations on the square, circle and swastika. Later on, these symbols became simplified into abstract hieroglyphics, which were composed of lines that no longer resembled specific objects. In addition to being used to communicate ideas, Runic letter images were considered so powerful and magical that they were inscribed into tools, weapons, rocks, altars and personal items. In addition, from these earliest of days, these magical markings were inscribed into wooden pieces that were thrown down and "read" as an early form of fortune telling.

The Runic alphabet is one of the oldest forms of writing. It is made up of straight lines that cross and break. Each letter, or Rune, has an intrinsic meaning in addition to its use for writing. For example, the first Rune "Fehu" is an actual word meaning cattle. What we now know as the Runic alphabet has developed from two different sources – literate and magical. Runes as we know them are formed from three main alphabets. The Teutonic, which has twenty-four letters, the Anglo Saxon which has thirty-two and the Scandinavian which has sixteen, but it is the Teutonic alphabet that we tend to use for divination today. Many Runic characters bear a resemblance to Latin letters, although they have few curves due to the fact that their design is suitable for carving with a knife.

These different alphabets are referred to as "Futharks", a word which comes from the first six letters of the Runic alphabet in the same way that the word "alphabet" comes from the first two words of the Greek alpha and beta or the Hebrew aleph and bayt. The Elder Futhark is basically the Teutonic alphabet, while the Younger Futhark contains only sixteen Runes, as in the Scandinavian set. There are many variations in the names given to individual Runes and there are also variations in the exact shape of certain Runes. The Elder Futhark is divided into three groups or "Aettir", and each Rune has an assigned place in the alphabet.

# The Aettir

The word Aett means eight, and Aettir is the plural, meaning eights. Each Aett, is named for a Norse god, the first being Freya's Aett, the second being Hagal's Aett and the third being Tyr's Aett. The following are the Runes contained in each Aett:

### *Freya's Aett*

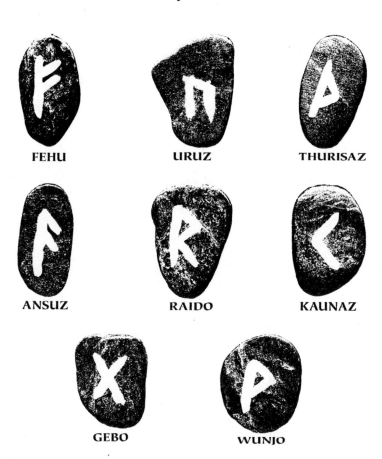

FEHU      URUZ      THURISAZ

ANSUZ      RAIDO      KAUNAZ

GEBO      WUNJO

## *Hagal's Aett*

**HAGALAZ**

**NAUTHIZ**

**ISA**

**JERA**

**EIHWAZ**

**PERTHO**

**ALGIZ**

**SOWELO**

*Tyr's Aett*

**TIWAZ**

**BERKANO**

**EHWAZ**

**MANNAZ**

**LAGUZ**

**INGUZ**

**OTHILA**

**DAGAZ**

There is a link between the picture, the letter and the sound that each Rune represents. Runes are more properly glyphs (hieroglyphics) rather than simple alphabetic characters, but at this distance in time we cannot be completely sure what the individual glyphs are meant to show. As time passed, the shape of some of the Runes changed. Most sources use the Germanic names for the Runes, while the Anglo Saxon is often given in brackets. The difference in meaning under the two systems for the names takes information from the two languages, and this in turn adds to our understanding of the Runes because the Anglo Saxon names are much closer to modern English and thus more accessible to us. Knowing how English developed can help us to understand the Runes. For example, the "g" in Old English often becomes the letter "y" in Modern English, "a" often becomes "o" and "ae" becomes "a". Using those rules we can look at the names of the Anglo Saxon Runes and make more sense of them. For example, "Rad" becomes "road" - a highly suitable name for a Rune that is connected with travel.

**Ancient Magic in the Runes**
According to mythology, the Runic alphabet was discovered by the god Odin while he hung head down for nine days and nights from Yggdrasil (the World Tree that supports the universe), upon which he had spied the Rune stones; he fell from the tree, crying and filled with knowledge. Each Runic character is connected with a deity from Scandinavian mythology and so contains in it a sequence of meanings derived from the deity's connections and relationships.

As well as changes in the names and symbols that developed over a period of time, there was also a change of attitude towards Runes. The Saxons renamed the Runes, breaking their links with the pagan gods but still permitting their use. In later years the Christian Church sought to eradicate the Runes, due to the fear that the Runes were much more than a mere alphabet and that they contained magic within their symbols. The word "Rune" is derived from the Old Norse and Old English "run" and the Gothic "runa", meaning a secret thing or a mystery. Their reputation for divinatory tools was enhanced when the Christian Church claimed they were used for casting magic spells and communicating with the devil. In recent years the popularity of Runes increased with the books of J.R.R. Tolkien, who used a form of Runes as "dwarfish" writing.

Nowadays, the Runes are used as a method of divination similar to the Tarot or I Ching. As with the Tarot, different meanings can be ascribed to Runes that fall in the reverse position. Due to their symmetrical shape, not all Runes can be read in reversed positions, so some Rune readers prefer not to differentiate between upright and reversed Runes. Runes can be made from any material, although most readers choose to use wood or stone.

# The Story of the Runes

### An Historical Overview

It is believed that the Runes originally derived from a northern Etruscan alphabet, which originated among peoples who dwelt in northern Italy and who spread into south central Europe. The earliest forms of Runic writing developed amongst people who were living in Bohemia. At some point, the idea of carving meaningful symbols traveled northward along the river routes to the lands in northern Europe and Scandinavia.

Pre-Runic symbols have been found in various Bronze Age rock carvings, mainly in Sweden, some of which are easily identifiable in later alphabets, while others represent ideas and concepts that have been incorporated into the names of the Runes. Rune figures can be found chiseled into rocks throughout areas that were inhabited by Germanic tribes. These people shared a common religion and culture and their mythology was passed on through an oral tradition. The people of Northern Europe used the Rune script until well into the Middle Ages. In addition to a written alphabet, Runes also served as a system of symbols used for magic and divination, so in this way the process of writing became a magical act.

When Christianity reached this area of the world, the development of the Nordic mythologies was brought to a close. However, the Vikings colonized Iceland where Christianity was a much weaker influence, and where it was possible to preserve the pre-Christian myths, and so it was in Iceland that they were first written down. The Roman alphabets became the preferred script of most of Europe between the thirteenth and sixteenth centuries, and so Rune writing fell into disuse. Interest in the Runes began to rise again in the seventeenth century, but the Christian Church soon banned them. Runes have now been rediscovered as a symbolic system and they have now become very popular as an accurate means of divination.

### Runic History in Detail

It is clear is that the Runes have always performed two functions, the first being a medium of containing, conveying and imparting information through inscribed symbols - as per any form of writing, and the second being for the purposes of divination and magic.

Before the Germanic peoples of Western Europe possessed a true alphabet, pictorial symbols were carved into stones. About 3,500 stone monuments in Europe, mainly concentrated in Sweden and Norway, are claimed to have been inscribed with Runic types of pictures, symbols and signs. The earliest of these writings date from about 1300 BC, and it is likely that they were linked to sun and fertility cults. The names given to the Runes indicate that a certain power was ascribed to them. The most famous users of the Runes were the Vikings who inscribed them everywhere that they went.

The name Rune means a secret thing or a mystery. When the high chieftains and wise counselors of Anglo-Saxon England met, they called their secret deliberations "Ruenes". When Bishop Wulfila translated the Bible into fourth century Gothic, he rendered St. Mark's "the mystery of the kingdom of God" and used the word, runa to mean mystery.

When the Greek historian Herodotus traveled around the area of the Black Sea, he encountered descendants of Scythian tribesmen who crawled under blankets, smoked themselves into a stupor, and then cast marked sticks in the air and "read" them when they fell. These sticks were used as a kind of Runic form of divination. By 100AD the Runes were already becoming widely known on the European Continent.

The most explicit surviving description of how the Runes were used comes from the Roman historian, Tacitus. Writing in 98 AD about practices prevalent among the Germanic tribes, he reports:

*"To divination and casting of lots they pay attention beyond any other people. Their method of casting lots is a simple one: they cut a branch from a fruit bearing tree and divide it into small pieces which they mark with certain distinctive signs (notae) and scatter at random onto a white cloth. Then, the priest of the community, if the lots are consulted publicly, or the father of the family, if it is done privately, after invoking the gods and with eyes raised to the heaven, picks up three pieces, one at a time, and interprets them according to the signs previously marked upon them."*

(Germania, Ch. X)

Runic letters were used to foretell the future by casting and they were also inscribed into tools, weapons and other items. Runic letters were also used by the clergy as an alternative to the Latin alphabet.

According to Norse belief the Runes were given to Odin, the father of creation. By means of the Runes he could communicate with his people; giving them warnings, blessings and also curses for their enemies.

Clearly, right from the start the Runes were regarded as sacred and thus treated with respect and dignity.

The Runic alphabet appears to have been derived from two distinct sources. The first is considered to be Swedish where pre-Runic symbols have been found in various Bronze Age carvings, while a second case been made for a Latin and Greek derivation of the Runic alphabet. The roots of the Runes are still argued over amongst scholars. The strongest evidence appears to point towards a North Italic origin. There are close parallels between the forms of the letters used in that area, in addition to the variable direction of the writing. Both Latin and Italic scripts derive from the Etruscan alphabet, which explains why so many Runes resemble Roman letters. This would place the creation of the Futhark sometime before the first century BC, when the Italic scripts were being absorbed and replaced by the Latin alphabet. Linguistic and phonetic analysis points to an even earlier inception date, perhaps as far back as 200 BC. As time went on, Runes became standardized throughout Europe, although in some places the Runes numbered as few as sixteen or as many as thirty-six, but twenty-four of these formed the basic Runes or Futhark. The Anglo Saxons are credited with spreading the Runes throughout Europe.

The Common Germanic Futhark (alphabet) remained in use among most of the Germanic peoples until approximately the fifth century AD. It was at about this time that the first changes in the Futhark emerged on Frisian soil. The fifth and sixth centuries were a time of great changes for the Frisian language, in which many vowels shifted in their sounds while new phonemes were added. This necessitated the expansion of the Rune row, and in this first expansion four new Runestaves were added to represent the new sounds in the Frisian language. The changes in the Frisian language also represented many of the changes that would be seen in Old English. Starting in the eighth century, yet more Runestaves were added. It must be pointed out though, that some of these staves are not properly Runes, but "pseudo-Runes." In the eighth century the Old Norse language also went through changes. Sounds shifted, some ceased to be used, while others were added. Old Norse speakers reduced the size of the Rune row from twenty-four to sixteen. As some sounds ceased being used, the Runes representing them also fell out of use. Similarly, the sounds of some Runes were taken over by others, resulting in those Runes ceasing to be used as well.

Though we speak of the Younger Futhark as if there is only one, in reality there were two different Norse Futharks - the Danish and the Norwegian-Swedish. As might be expected of a script that often uses a single stave to represent several different sounds, the sixteen Rune row apparently proved impractical for writing. Eventually a system of "pointed Runes" developed, whereby a Runestave that denoted several sounds would have a point or dot added to it in a particular place to differentiate between sounds. This appears to have started in Denmark and spread outward from there. Unlike the Anglo-Frisian Rune row, the Younger Futhark did not fall completely out of use, so the Runes were being used well into the Middle Ages; indeed, so much so that Iceland eventually banned their use.

From the ninth through to the twelfth centuries, the Runes were carried to Anglo-Saxon England and to Iceland. Rune carvings have been found as far afield as Russia, Constantinople, the Orkney Islands, Greenland and (some believe), the North American continent. Later, shaped by the tribal wisdom of northern Europe, the Viking Runes emerged. With the onset of Christianity the Runes were seen as demonic and as letters of the devil. By

800 AD there was such persecution of the Runes and their users that their use slowly began to wane.

The situation was different in England where Runes were not actively suppressed by the church and where they appeared in Christian documents. They fell out of use by the ninth century when they were overtaken by the Latin script even for the purposes of inscriptions, although they were still being used (albeit in a more limited way) in Scandinavia and Iceland.

In 1486 the Malleus Maleficarum by Henricus Institoris (Heinrich Institoris Kraemer) and Jacobus Sprenger (Johann Sprenger) set off the witch-hunt that was to burn throughout Europe. This book was basically a guide to witch-hunting and it specifically mentions Runes:

"Or even let us conceive that if they superstitiously employ natural things, as, for example, by writing down certain characters or unknown names of some kind, and that then they use these Runes for restoring a person to health, or for inducing friendship, or with some useful end, and not at all for doing any damage or harm, in such cases, it may be granted, I say, that there is no express invocation of demons; nevertheless it cannot be that these spells are employed without a tacit invocation, wherefore all such charms must be judged to be wholly unlawful."

Despite this, the Runes did not disappear. The Elizabethan magician, John Dee, worked with Runes, and mystical works about Rune interpretation and magic continued to be written.

Calendars known as Primstave, or Runstaf were used to mark church holy days as well as times for planting and harvesting, and these persisted beyond the medieval period in Scandinavia. An indication of their enduring popularity is evident from a seventeenth-century inscription on the choir wall of a church in Oland, Sweden, which says, "The pastor of the parish should know how to read Runes and write them." Among the country people of Dalarna, a remote region of western Sweden, survival of knowledge of the Runes has continued into the twentieth century. In Norway, among the Lapps of Finnmark in the country's far North, drums that have Runes painted on them are still in use today by local Shamans.

Until the seventeenth century Runes were in such common use that they were found on everything from coins to coffins. In some places their use was actually sanctioned by the Church. Even the common people knew simple Runic spells, and Runes were frequently consulted on matters of both public and private interest. However, in 1639 they were banned by the Church along with many magical arts in an effort to "drive the devil out of Europe". By this time, Runes were primarily of interest to antiquarians but during the "Enlightenment", interest in the Runes was rekindled. Scholars transcribed the Runic poems and made the first studies into the Runes and Runic inscriptions. By the nineteenth century many scholars were studying the Runes.

In 1902 the Austrian journalist and author Guido Von List suffered a period of blindness following a cataract operation. It was during this period that he experienced a vision in which an alternative set of Runes were revealed to him, and he published details of this in his 1908 book, "The Secrets of the Runes". Von List was a German nationalist and his Runes were linked with the mythological and racial ideology that was Armanism. He founded the Thule Society, which was an occult and right-wing political organization, in order to propagate his views. In recent history the Runes were revived by German researchers connected with the Nazi movement in the 1920s and 1930s.

Though occultism was officially banned under the Nazis and many leading German occultists were imprisoned, key members of the party had a strong interest in the occult. These were principally Himmler and the official philosopher of the party, Alfred Rosenberg. Hitler was less interested, but he knew the value of symbols and incorporated ancient symbols of power such as Roman, Scandinavian or ancient Germanic ones into the flags, staves, emblems and uniform badges of the time. The works of Von List therefore found favor and it was his Armanen Runes, which were adopted by the party for a number of their badges and emblems.

The Tiwaz Rune served as the badge of the Hitler Youth movement. The Rune, Sowelo or Sigil as it was known to the Nazis, was linked with the German word "sieg" (victory) and a doubled version was used as the logo of the SS. The lightning flash emblem of the British Union of Fascists was also inspired by the Sigil Rune. During the Nazi period Runes were used throughout Germany - even on tombstones.

After the Second World War, as a result of their association with Nazism, the Runes fell into disfavor, and very little was written about them until the 1950s and 1960s. Interest revived slowly as organizations such as the Odinic Rite and the Ring of Troth were formed to further the study of the Northern mysteries, and to pursue the religion known as Asatru.

It was not until the middle of the 1980s, with the widespread appeal of the "New Age" movement and the revival of Pagan religions (especially the Asatru movement) that the Runes regained their popularity as both a divinatory system and a tool for self-awareness. However, as early as 1937 Runes gained ground in the UK with the publication of JRR Tolkein's "The Hobbit". Runes were used in the map and cover illustrations of the book. He continued to use Runes as "dwarfish" writing in his other books. Runes appear on the title pages of "The

Lord of the Rings" which was published in 1954. Tolkien is said to have taken his Runes from a Viking long boat discovered in the river Thames. In the 1970s heavy metal bands such as Led Zeppelin used Runes as illustrations on album covers, and accusations of Satanism led to Runes being associated with black magic during this period.

By the mid 1980s a large number of Rune books were being published. Ralph Blum's book, which was accompanied by a complimentary set of Runes, started the trend, and it has continued to be the best seller in the genre. Blum drew very little upon the original lore: he even created his own order for the Rune row rather than relying upon the traditional Futhark. Blum also introduced the blank Rune, although he does not claim responsibility for inventing it, but says it was included in a set of Runes he purchased in Surrey. Many regard it as showing a misunderstanding of the Runes and upsetting their balance. Runes are now popular as a divinatory system and many people in recent years have been attempting to reclaim their long history.

# The Mythology of the Runes

All systems of divination stem from somewhere, and every one of them has a mythology, religion, philosophy or belief system behind it. It is the instinctive fear of these pagan ideas that leads those who sincerely believe in one of our modern religions to vilify these systems.

Among those who learn the various divinations, some are fascinated by the stories that underpin them, while others view them as an irrelevance that gets in the way of their desire to use the system in question. However, without knowing where the signs, symbols and archetypes stem from, how can anyone hope to understand their true meaning? The Runes are so heavily dependent upon an ancient belief system, complete with a full cast of characters and a variety of occult meanings, that it is essential to have at least some idea of where their images are coming from.

## The Believers

Some hundreds of years before the Christian era, the Germanic people settled over much of Central Europe and they lived in what is now modern Scandinavia and Germany. Although covering a wide area they shared a culture, and their myths were passed on through oral tradition. With the advent of Christianity, the Northern and

Teutonic mythologies faced an end in their development. However, when the Vikings colonized Iceland (which was less influenced by Christianity), their ancestral religion became preserved, thus it is in Iceland that the myths were first put down in writing. The tenth century book "Eddas" offers thorough descriptions of cosmogony, mythology and the traditions of the Teutonic and Nordic tribes. These early peoples were called Asatru - an Icelandic word meaning "those of the Aesir". Although replaced by Christianity, their religion was kept alive in Iceland and Lapland into the nineteenth century and it was revived in the 1970s. The Asatru worship the deities of the ancient Norse and Germanic peoples.

The Asatru believed in the "Nine Noble Virtues" of Courage, Honor, Loyalty, Hospitality, Industriousness, Truth, Perseverance, Self-discipline and Self-reliance. They revered their ancestors and their "honored dead", and they also revered nature and the spirits of the world. They held Hospitality and Truth to be above reproach. The Asatru held four major holy celebrations, which occurred in autumn, at the beginning of winter, in midwinter and at the beginning of spring.

*NB:* The honored dead were those who had been killed in battle rather than those who simply died a natural death.

The gods were not seen as remote creatures but as beings who exerted an influence on the world and whom they considered to be prone to the same flaws as humans. They were subject to the universal laws and they could not escape Wyrd, the cosmic justice that forced them to face the consequences of their deeds. Death would come to them all at the end, particularly at Ragnarok - the Twilight of the Gods.

## Words and Language

We do not have to go back very far into history for spelling to be a moveable feast and sometimes you do not have to go back at all. For instance, this book has been produced in American English rather than British English, because it will "travel" better. You may notice that words like behavior, traveling, instill, fulfillment, center, symbolize and criticize are spelled differently from their British equivalents of behaviour, centre, traveling, instil, fulfilment, symbolise and criticise.

The spelling associated with the Runes and their history stretches across many centuries and languages, so there are many variations in the way these mythical characters and places are spelled, and indeed among the Runes within each type of Futhark. In this book, I have made my choices and kept them reasonably consistent, although there are some extremely obvious slight variations. For instance, Muspell is sometimes referred to as Muspellheim - heim being home or place of. Heim still means home or area in modern German. In addition, there is no distinction between common and proper nouns in German, so all nouns are written with a capital letter - as are the words Rune and Aettir in this book.

## The Beliefs

At the beginning of time there was Muspell, which was the realm of Fire. Only the Fire Giants could tolerate the light and heat of Muspell. It was guarded by Sutr, who was armed with a flaming sword. It was believed that at the end of the world he and his companions would destroy the gods and that the world would be consumed by fire. Outside Muspell was an empty land called Ginnungap. To the north was a land of dark and cold called Nifelheim. In this world there were eleven rivers that flow from a great well, and these frozen rivers occupied Ginnungap.

When the wind, ice and cold met the heat of Muspell in the center of Ginnungap, a place of light, air and warmth was born and thawing drops of ice appeared. The Frost Giant, Ymir, slept beneath the melting ice. Under his left arm grew pair of male and female giants. One of the male's legs begot a son with the female. The melting frost became a cow, Audhumla, from whose udders ran four rivers of milk that fed Ymir. After a day spent licking ice she freed a man's hair, after two days she freed his head and on the third she freed him completely. This man was called Bury. Bury married Bestla, the daughter of a giant, and they had three sons called Odin, Vili and Ve'.

The three brothers killed Ymir and carried him to the middle of Ginnungap, creating the world (Midgard), from his body. His blood became the sea and lakes and his skull the cover of the sky. His brains became the clouds, his skeleton the mountains, his teeth and jaw, rocks and pebbles, and his hair the trees. The maggots from his flesh became dwarves who looked like humans and had human understanding, but who lived in the earth. The sparks and burning embers from Muspell gave light and the stars were named and set in their paths.

Midgard was surrounded by an ocean. Odin, Vili and Ve' gave lands to the friendly giants who were called the Etin. The Etin created a man and woman from two trees. Odin filled them with spirit and life, while Vili gave them understanding and movement, and Ve' gave them clothing and names. The man was named Ask (Ash) and the woman Embla (Elm), and they are the ancestors of all humans. The brothers then built Asgard, the home of the gods. Odin married Frigga, the daughter of the giant Fjirgvin.

The world tree, Yggdrasil, rose from the center of Asgard with its branches reaching over Asgard. One of its roots reaches into the underworld Hel (also Hell or Helheim). Another led to the world of the Frost Giants and a third to the world of humans. Underneath the tree is the Urda well, which was guarded by the Norns, the goddesses of fate who used the well to irrigate the roots of Yggdrasil.

The Norns were three sisters or goddesses of fate who had some link with the older, pastoral gods - the Vanir. They represented time itself, so Urd, the Norn of the past, was depicted as an ancient crone who constantly looked back to the "good old days". The young and lively, Verdandi, Norn of the present, looked alert, while Skuld, the Norn of the future was mistily pictured in a veil, and holding an unopened scroll. The Norns were occasionally dictated to by an elemental force called Wyrd who some scribes recorded as a person, representing as their mother. The Norns wove the web of Wyrd (or fate), which sets out the fate of gods and humans. This web was so huge that it covered the known world. The three witches in Macbeth and even the word, weird - with its strange "e-before-i" spelling - still linger in our consciousness.

The wells of Hvregelmer and Mimir's well also fed Yggdrasil. The dragon or serpent, Nidhog, lay in Hvregelmer and gnawed on the roots of the tree. Mimir's well was the well of wisdom, and it was guarded by Mimir. Odin gave his right eye for a drink of the water from Mimir's well.

The knowledge of the Runes was originally in the possession of Mimir. He obtained this knowledge from the underground fountain which lay beneath the middle root of the World Tree and which he guarded. For nine days and nine nights Odin hung upside down from the World Tree. He had been pierced by a spear and during that time he had no food or drink. The days dragged out and nine nights passed, then Odin saw the shapes of the Runes deep in the tree's roots. Crying out, he caught up the Runes and fell from the Tree. Then Besla's brother gave him a drink from the fountain. He also received nine of the songs that were the basis of the magic that lies in the application of the power of words and of the Runes over spiritual and natural forces. The Runes then became a channel for the protection of the gods, which enabled them to assist their worshippers when in danger and distress.

The Runes of Victory could stop weapons and make those who Odin loved proof against the sword. Other Runes had powers that controlled the elements, gave speech to the mute, freed the limbs from bonds, protected against witchcraft, took strength from the love potion prepared by another man's wife, helped in childbirth and healed the sick, gave wisdom and knowledge and extinguished enmity. Odin taught the knowledge of the Runes to his own clan. Dinn taught it to the elves, Dvalinn taught the dwarves, æsvinr taught the giants. Heimdal taught the Runes to humanity, in particular to certain noble families, who were said to possess the power of the Runes as a gift of the gods.

The gods built a bridge made from a rainbow between Asgard and Midgard and they rode across it daily. It was guarded by the god Heimdal who it was said, slept lighter than a bird, could see one hundred travel-days in each direction, and had such sharp ears that he could hear grass and wool grow. It is said that the bridge will collapse when the Frost Giants ride over it at Ragnarok.

The gods were divided into two groups - the Aesirs and the Vanirs. The Vanir, or earth gods, symbolize riches, fertility and fecundity. They were associated with the earth and the sea. The most important Gods of the Vanir were Njord, Freyr, Aegir and Freya. The Aesir, or sky gods, symbolized power, wisdom and war. They were long-lived but not immortal. The Aesir lived in Asgard in two buildings - Gladsheim for the gods and Vingolf for the goddesses. The Vanirs were the older race of gods and they were also masters of magic. The Vanirs lived in Vanaheim.

At one time there was a clash between the two sets of gods. This meant that the Aesirs, led by Odin and Frigga on one side, and the Vanirs, led by Heimdal, Freyr and Freya went to war with each other. The spark that ignited this war was an attempted murder by the Aesirs of the oracle and sorcerer Gullveig, who was said to be concerned only with her love for gold. The Aesirs burnt her to ashes three times but each time she recovered. The Vanirs, angered at her treatment by the Aesirs had prepared for war.

Eventually peace came and the gods exchanged hostages. The Vanir sent Njord and his children, Freya and Freyr, to Asgard, while the Aesirs sent Honir and Mimir to Vanaheim. Honir caused the Vanirs to be suspicious; so, believing they had been cheated, they beheaded him and sent his head back to the Aesirs. The dispute was eventually resolved and the Vanirs became assimilated, and so all the gods continued to live in Asgard.

Odin was the leader of the gods. Thor was the god of thunder and Loki was a giant who became an Aesir by adoption, and thus a blood brother of Odin. Loki was a trickster. Odin's son, Baldur, settled disputes.

Baldur had a dream in which his life was a threatened. His mother, Frigga forced the elements of fire, water, metal and earth in addition to stones, birds and animals to swear not to harm him. Loki discovered that the only thing that could harm Baldur was mistletoe, so created a set of arrows with it. He took these to the blind god, Hodor, who was Baldur's brother, and directed his aim so that Baldur was killed. Baldur did not die in battle, so he was sent to Hel. Odin begged Baldur's release. Hel, who was Loki's daughter, said that if everything in the world (whether it was alive or dead) wept for Baldur he could return. The only one not to respond to the god's plea was the giantess Thokk who was actually Loki in disguise. The Aesir captured Loki, and as punishment for this and other crimes, chained him beneath a serpent that dripped venom onto him and left him in great pain.

## The Future of the Gods - and of the World

When Mimir ceases to guard his well, Yggdrasil's root will start to rot, and the Nidhog dragon/serpent will gnaw through the root at Hvregelmer's Well. Odin's sacrificed eye will see the coming of three years of endless winter followed by Ragnarok. One of Yggdrasil's branches will break and fall, striking Jormungand (the world serpent), which immediately will let go of its tail.

*NB:* Some traditions suggest that Jormungand is a turtle and that the tree and the world are all perched on its back. The popular fantasy books by Terry Pratchett use this myth as their basis.

The Hel ship, Naglfar, will become visible in the mist. The wolves Skoll and Manegarm will move closer and closer to Sun and Moon. Loki will be released by giants and Nidhog will leave the roots of Yggdrasil and head toward Asgard. As the giants march on Asgard, Heimdal will sound a warning and Loki will lead the monsters and giants in their last great battle. Many of the gods will die and the World Tree will fall down and burn. Some Aesir will escape in Frey's ship. Midgard will be destroyed by fire and sink back into the sea. Finally, the earth will re-emerge from the sea and seven sons of the dead Aesir will return to Asgard and rule the universe.

## The Nine Worlds

Before leaving this chapter, we ought to get to grips with the nine worlds that make up the created universe and which are all connected by the roots and branches of the World Tree, Yggdrasil, as well as being subject to the web of Wyrd. Odin traveled freely through these worlds on the back of his mighty eight-legged stallion, Sleipnir. Ancient sorcerers could also travel on dream journeys through these worlds, using the Runes as talismans, amulets or as keys to other realms of existence.

Midgard was the world of mortal humans - our world.

To the north lay Nifelheim, which was the world of the serpent or dragon, Nidhog.

Jotunheim was the world of the Giants and this lay on the outer fringes of creation.

Muspell lay to the south and was the world of fire.

Vanaheim was the original world of the old Vanir gods.

Alfheim was the world of the Elves.

Swartalfheim was the world of the Dark Elves.

Helheim was the lowest realm; the home of the dishonored dead - or those who did not die in battle.

Asgard was the highest realm and the home of the Aesir gods, also the location of Valhalla, the home of Odin and the honored dead - a kind of Nirvana.

# The Link between the gods and the Runes

This is where the Runes connect with the gods and the sagas. The alternative names are given in brackets. Although it is against tradition, I have numbered each Rune throughout this book in order to help you locate them when you need to do so.

*1   .   Fehu – Aesir/Audhumla (the Cow)*
The Aesir is the collective name for the Old Norse gods of the family of which Odin was the patriarch. The gods are strong; they are also beautiful and larger than ordinary people – a race of super-humans. Although they live longer than humans they are not immortal. Each of them holds a different sort of knowledge. They are the gods of consciousness and the sky.
Audhumla is the cow that fed Ymir with her milk.

*2.     Uruz – Vanir/Ymir*
The Vanir are the older race of gods and the gods of earth, biological life and the unconscious.
Ymir is the Frost Giant who slept under the ice.

3.    *Thurisaz – Thor/The Race of Giants*
Thor (Thirr, Thunar, Donar) is the god of thunder and lightening, agriculture and craftsmanship. He is also the god of strength and defense. Thor is the champion of the gods and the protector of humanity. He wears a magic belt that can double his strength and also a pair of gauntlets, which allow him to wield his mighty hammer, Mjolnir. He drives a chariot pulled by two giant goats. Thor can change his size, and although he can be hasty in his judgment he makes a reliable friend and battle companion.

4    *Ansuz – Odin*
Odin (Woden, Wotan, Odhinn) is the principal god of the Aesir, although he began as a minor deity of night storms. Two ravens, called Thought and Memory, accompany him. Odin lives on nothing but wine, as his two wolves consume all food he is offered. He rides an eight-legged horse, Sleipnir, and he is married to the goddess Frigga. Odin is a god of the dead, of warriors, of weather, of war and of magic. He is also a healer, shaman and teacher.

5.    *Raido - The Norns (fates)*
The Norns (or Nornir - the old plural form of the word) are the three fates of Norse myth, and they represent the past, present and future.

6.    *Kaunaz – Freya/Dwarves/Heimdal*
Freya (Freyja) is a member of the Vanir who lives with the Aesir. She owns a falcon cloak, takes the form of a dove and rides in a chariot drawn by two cats or a boar. As the leader of the Valkyries, she takes half of those slain in battle and is associated with death and sexuality. She weeps tears of gold, which later become amber.

The dwarves were originally maggots but they have been given intelligence by the gods.

Heimdal was the son of Odin and a friend to mankind. He revealed the secret of the Runes to his mortal descendents.

### 7.      Gebo – Odin/Freya

Odin (Woden, Wotan, Odhinn) is the principal god of the aesir, although he began as a minor deity of night storms. As mentioned in item 4 above, two ravens called Thought and Memory accompany him. Odin lives on nothing but wine, as his wolves consume all food he is offered. He rides an eight-legged horse, Sleipnir, and he is married to the goddess Frigga. Odin is a god of the dead, of warriors, weather, war and magic. He is also a healer, shaman and a teacher.

### 8.      Wunjo – Freyr/Elves

Freyr (Frey) is the brother consort of Freya. He is the god of wealth and peace and contentment. Freyr owns the boar, Gullinbursti, the ship, Skidbladnir and a magic sword that moves by itself through the air. He rules over the land of the Light Elves and is also the god of sensuality, fertility, growth, abundance, bravery, horses, boars, joy, happiness, rain and weather. He is the protector of oaths and also of ships and sailors.

The Elves are divided into three races - Light, Dark and Black. They cause sickness and their arrows can cause strokes and paralysis. They are wise magicians who frequently take an interest in individual humans. The Elves are unpredictable and they take both offense and pleasure in the slightest things.

### 9.    Hagalaz – Ymir/Urd

Ymir is the primal being created by the first meeting of fire and ice in Ginnungap. He is the first Frost Giant from whose slain body the world was created.

Urd is the eldest of the three Norns.

### 10.   Nauthiz – Nornir/Etins

The Nornir are the three fates of Norse myth and they represent the past, present and future.

The Etin are a race of giants known for their strength and usually friendly towards the gods.

### 11.   Isa – Rime Thursur

The Rime Thursur are a race of Frost Giants who are characterized by great strength and age. They are renowned for their witlessness and strength.

### 12.   Jera – Freyr/Baldur/Hodur/Loki

Freyr (Frey) is the brother consort of Freya. (Also see item 8 above). He is the god of wealth, peace and contentment. Freyr owns the boar Gullinbursti, the ship Skidbladnir and a magic sword that moves by itself through the air. He rules over the land of the Light Elves and is also the god of sensuality, fertility, growth,abundance, bravery, horses, boars, joy, happiness and rain. He is the protector of oaths, ships and sailors.

Baldur the Beautiful and Hodor the Blind are sons of Odin. Hodor was tricked by Loki into killing Baldur with a shaft of mistletoe.

Loki was the giant god of thunder who became an Aesir by adoption. He became Odin's blood brother, but he was a trickster who caused Odin and others much trouble.

*13. Eihwaz – Idhunna/Ullr*

Idhunna (Idunna) is the goddess of eternal life and youth and the keeper of the golden apples of youth and immortality.

Ullr (Uller, Uller, Ull, Wulder) is the winter god of archery, skiing and yew magic. He is the stepson of Thor and a member of the Vanir. At one time he was considered to be as important as Odin, and in winter he is the ruler of Asgard.

*14. Pertho – The Norns*

The Norns are the three fates of Norse myth, and they represent the past, the present and the future.

*15. Algiz – Valkyrijur (The Valkyries)*

The Valkyries (Valkyrja) were sent into battle by Odin to select those who would go to Valhalla. They were women who were trained in battle and war magic and they would enter the fray with the warriors. They take the forms of ravens and swans, they choose among the slain and they bring fertility to the earth.

*16. Sowelo – Sol/Baldur/Hodur*

Sol (Sunna, Gull) is a sun goddess.

Baldur the Beautiful and Hodor the Blind are sons of Odin. Hodor was tricked by Loki into killing Baldur with a shaft of mistletoe.

*17. Tiwaz – Tyr/Mani*

Tyr, (Tiu, Tiw, Ziu) is the one-handed god of defense and victory, and he is known as the bravest of all the gods. He is the giver of victory in battles against the odds and he is never deceitful. Tyr presides over law. Sometimes he is referred to as the son of Odin and at other times as an older god that preceded Odin.

Mani is the god of the Moon and together with his sister, the Sun, he was placed in the sky by the Aesir.

### 18.  Berkano - Frigga/ Nerthus/Hel

Frigg (Frigga, Frija) knows the fate of all men and gods although she does not prophesy. She is married to Odin and they have six sons and one daughter. She is the goddess of childbirth and an aspect of fate. She also represents married sexuality.

Nerthus (Erda) is the primal earth mother. She is the oldest of the goddesses and she considered to be a goddess of fertility. The worship of Nerthus was centered in Denmark. Nerthus lived in a grove on a sacred island, and once a year traveled the land in a wagon bringing a season of peace and plenty. When she was tired she returned to her island and was bathed in a lake by slaves who were later drowned.

Hel (Hela, Hella) is the giant goddess of death and the underworld, which shares her name, Hel. She rules the home of the dead who have not died in battle. Odin, who gave her authority over life in the nine worlds on condition that she shared her provisions with those sent to her, sent her into Nifelheim. This terrifying apparition is half blackened and hideous corpse and half a vibrant and beautiful woman.

### 19.  Ehwaz  - Freyja/Freyr/Aclis/Sleipnir

The Aclis are twin gods, said to be the sons of the sky god.

Sleipnir is the mighty eight-legged horse ridden by Odin.

### 20.  Mannaz - Heimdal/Odin

On the first day a boat drifted to the shores of mankind containing the boy Heimdal. He slept on a sheaf of corn, surrounded by treasures and tools. Raised by humans he taught them how to kindle fire and instructed them in Runic wisdom and crafts. When he died, his ship took him back to the gods where he regained eternal youth and was taken into Asgard. He stands at the gate of the Bifrost Bridge and is a handsome, fierce warrior. He has super-sight and super-hearing. At Ragnarok he will blow the Gjall Horn in warning and it will be heard throughout the nine worlds.

### 21.  Laguz  - Njord/Baldur/Nerthus/Skadi/Ullr

Njord (Nhord) is the god of seafaring. He controls the wind and stills the sea and fire. He was married to the giantess Skadi, who chose him for his beautiful feet, mistakenly thinking he was Baldur. As they could not agree on where to live, they split up. He has ten children, amongst them Freyr and Freya and is Frigg's brother.

Baldur (Baldr, Balder) is the son of Odin and Frigga, who was killed by an arrow of mistletoe shot by the blind god Hodor, who had been tricked by Loki. He was known as the shining god or bleeding god. He represents light, advice, reconciliation, beauty, wisdom, harmony, happiness and reincarnation. After Ragnarok he will return to rule as one of the new gods.

### 22.  Inguz  - Ing/Freyr

Ing is a fertility god of protection and the patron god of England and the Danes.

### 23.  Othila - Odin

As mentioned earlier, Odin (Woden, Wotan, Odhinn) is the principal god of the Aesir, although he began as a minor deity of night storms. Two ravens called Thought and Memory accompany him. Odin lives on nothing but wine, as his wolves consume all food he is offered. He rides an eight-legged horse, Sleipnir, and he is married to the goddess Frigga. Odin is a god of the dead, of warriors, weather, war and magic. He is also a healer, shaman and a teacher.

### 24.  Dagaz - Odin/Ostara/Loki/Heimdal

One of the Vanir, Ostara is the fertility goddess of the dawn and it is she who brings the spring. She is a friend to all children and she is said to have changed her pet bird into a rabbit in order to amuse them. The rabbit brought forth brightly colored eggs, which she gave to the children as gifts. The word "Easter" is derived from her name.

Loki was from the race of Giants. He tried to kill Odin and was the enemy of Heimdal.

### 25.  The Blank Rune - Wyrd

Wyrd was the cosmic force of justice that forced all the gods to face the consequences of their deeds. She was sometimes said to be the mother of the Norns. Wyrd wove a web of fate that covered the known world.

# The Rune Poems

Four Rune poems survive today, each of which lists the Runes and their names. The oldest is the Abecedarium Nordmanicum, which means "The Alphabet of the Northerners". The other three Rune poems are The Old English Rune Poem, The Old Norwegian Rune Poem and the Old Icelandic Rune Poem, which combined with Abecedarium Nordmanicum give us the meanings of the Runes as we use them today.

The oldest of these three Runes poems is The Old English Rune Poem. It is believed to date between the eighth and tenth century AD. This was nearly lost when the original manuscript was destroyed by fire in 1731 but fortunately, it had already been transcribed. This is the only poem that covers all twenty-four of the Runes of the Elder Futhark, as well as the Runes from the first expansion of the Anglo-Frisian Futhorc (Futhark). The Old Norwegian Rune Poem dates to the late twelfth or early thirteenth centuries. It is the only Rune poem that refers to Christ by name. The Old Icelandic Rune Poem is the youngest of the three, dating back only as far as the fifteenth century. Despite this, it sometimes appears to be the most heathen in sentiment of the three Rune poems and it has the most extensive references to Germanic mythology.

The three Rune poems are very similar, and verses within one poem are sometimes reflected by the other two. It seems likely that all three poems are descended from the same source. The similarities show that the ideas and images regarding the Runes were similar throughout the Germanic tribes.

The Rune Poems were a recitation of the names and "kennings" (associations) of the Runes, and presumably used as an aid in memorizing and transmitting the lore.

### The Abecedarium Nordmanicum

This is sometimes referred to as The Old Swiss Rune Poem. It was discovered in a manuscript written in the 9th century, written in High and Low German. The terms, "high" and "low" do not refer to a class or standard of ancient German, but the places from which they originated; High German originated in the more northerly areas of Germanic Europe and Low German from the south. The Abecedarium Nordmanicum relates to the Younger Futhark.

Fee first
Aurochs after
Thurs the third stave
The Ase is above him
Wheel is written last
Then cleaves cancre;
Hail has need;
Ice, year and sun.
Tiu, birch and man in the middle;
Water the bright
Yew holds all.

### The Icelandic Rune Poem

Wealth
source of discord among kinsmen

and fire of the sea
and path of the serpent.
Shower
lamentation of the clouds
and ruin of the hay-harvest
and abomination of the shepherd.
Giant
torture of women
and cliff-dweller
and husband of a giantess.
God
aged Gautr
and prince of Asgaror
and lord of Valhalla.
Riding
joy of the horsemen
and speedy journey
and toil of the steed.
Ulcer
disease fatal to children
and painful spot
and abode of mortification.
Hail
cold grain
and shower of sleet
and sickness of serpents. Constraint
grief of the bondmaid
and state of oppression
and toilsome work.
Ice
bark of rivers
and roof of the wave
and destruction of the doomed.
Plenty
boon to men

and good summer
and thriving crops.
Sun
shield of the clouds
and shining ray
and destroyer of ice.
Tyr
god with one hand
and leavings of the wolf
and prince of temples.
Birch
leafy twig
and little tree
and fresh young shrub.
Man
delight of man
and augmentation of the earth
and adorner of ships.
Water
eddying stream
and broad geysir
and land of the fish.
Yew
bent bow
and brittle iron
and giant of the arrow.

### *The Norwegian Rune Poem*

Wealth is a source of discord among kinsmen;
the wolf lives in the forest.
Dross comes from bad iron;
the reindeer often races over the frozen snow.
Giant causes anguish to women;
misfortune makes few men cheerful.
Estuary is the way of most journeys;

but a scabbard is of swords.
Riding is said to be the worst thing for horses;
Reginn forged the finest sword.
Ulcer is fatal to children;
death makes a corpse pale.
Hail is the coldest of grain;
Christ created the world of old.
Constraint gives scant choice;
a naked man is chilled by the frost.
Ice we call the broad bridge;
the blind man must be led.
Plenty is a boon to men;
I say that Frothi was generous.
Sun is the light of the world;
I bow to the divine decree.
Tyr is a one-handed god;
often has the smith to blow.
Birch has the greenest leaves of any shrub;
Loki was fortunate in his deceit.
Man is an augmentation of the dust;
great is the claw of the hawk.
A waterfall is a River that falls from a mountainside;
but ornaments are of gold.
Yew is the greenest of trees in winter;
it is wont to crackle when it burns.

### The Anglo-Saxon Rune Poem
Wealth is a comfort to all men;
yet must every man bestow it freely,
if he wish to gain honor in the sight of the Lord.
The aurochs is proud and has great horns;
it is a very savage beast and fights with its horns;
a great ranger of the moors, it is a creature of mettle.
The thorn is exceedingly sharp,
an evil thing for any knight to touch,

uncommonly severe on all who sit among them.
The mouth is the source of all language,
a pillar of wisdom and a comfort to wise men,
a blessing and a joy to every knight.
Riding seems easy to every warrior while he is indoors
and very courageous to him who traverses the high-roads
on the back of a stout horse.
The torch is known to every living man by its pale, bright flame;
it always burns where princes sit within.
Generosity brings credit and honor, which support one's dignity;
it furnishes help and subsistence
to all broken men who are devoid of aught else.
Bliss he enjoys who knows not suffering, sorrow nor anxiety,
and has prosperity, happiness, and a good enough house.
Hail is the whitest of grain;
it is whirled from the vault of heaven
and is tossed about by gusts of wind
and then it melts into water.
Trouble is oppressive to the heart;
yet often it proves a source of help and salvation
to the children of men, to everyone who heeds it betimes.
Ice is very cold and immeasurably slippery;
it glistens as clear as glass and most like to gems;
it is a floor wrought by the frost, fair to look upon.
Summer is a joy to men, when God, the holy King of Heaven,
suffers the earth to bring forth shining fruits
for rich and poor alike.

The yew is a tree with rough bark,
hard and fast in the earth, supported by its roots,
a guardian of flame and a joy upon an estate.
Peorth is a source of recreation and amusement to the
great,
where warriors sit blithely together in the
banqueting-hall.
The Eolh-sedge is mostly to be found in a marsh;
it grows in the water and makes a ghastly wound,
covering with blood every warrior who touches it.
The sun is ever a joy in the hopes of seafarers
when they journey away over the fishes' bath,
until the courser of the deep bears them to land.
Tiw is a guiding star; well does it keep faith with
princes;
it is ever on its course over the mists of night and
never fails.
The poplar bears no fruit; yet without seed it brings
forth suckers,
for it is generated from its leaves.
Splendid are its branches and gloriously adorned
its lofty crown, which reaches to the skies.
The horse is a joy to princes in the presence of
warriors.
A steed in the pride of its hoofs,
when rich men on horseback bandy words about it;
and it is ever a source of comfort to the restless.
The joyous man is dear to his kinsmen;
yet every man is doomed to fail his fellow,
since the Lord by his decree will commit the vile
carrion to the earth.
The ocean seems interminable to men,
if they venture on the rolling bark
and the waves of the sea terrify them
and the courser of the deep heeds not its bridle.

Ing was first seen by men among the East-Danes,
till, followed by his chariot,
he departed eastwards over the waves.
So the Heardingas named the hero.
An estate is very dear to every man,
if he can enjoy there in his house
whatever is right and proper in constant prosperity.
Day, the glorious light of the Creator, is sent by the
Lord;
it is beloved of men, a source of hope and happiness
to rich and poor,
and of service to all.
The oak fattens the flesh of pigs for the children of
men.
Often it traverses the gannet's bath,
and the ocean proves whether the oak keeps faith
in honorable fashion.
The ash is exceedingly high and precious to men.
With its sturdy trunk it offers a stubborn resistance,
though attacked by many a man.
Yr is a source of joy and honor to every prince and
knight;
it looks well on a horse and is a reliable equipment
for a journey.
Iar is a river fish and yet it always feeds on land;
it has a fair abode encompassed by water, where it
lives in happiness.
The grave is horrible to every knight,
when the corpse quickly begins to cool
and is laid in the bosom of the dark earth.
Prosperity declines, happiness passes away
and covenants are broken.

### The Havamal

The story of how the Runes were found is told in the poem Havamal, or "Words of the High One". The High One in this case is the god Odin, known as the "Allfather", and the "Leader of the gods".

> *Foolish is he who frets at night,*
> *And lies awake to worry*
> *A weary man when morning comes,*
> *He finds all as bad as before*

In order to gain wisdom and eloquence Odin had sacrificed one of his eyes, swapping it for a drink from Mimir's Well.

> *Wounded I hung on a wind-swept gallows*
> *For nine long nights,*
> *Pierced by a spear, pledged to Odin*
> *Offered myself to myself.*

After the story of how Odin discovered the Runes, the Havamal discusses preparation and use of the Runes.

> *Know how to cut them, know how to read them*
> *Know how to stain them, know how to prove them*
> *Know how to evoke them, know how to score them*
> *Know how to send them, know how to spend them*

The last section of the poem lists eighteen charms using Runes and the magical effects they produce.

> *I know a third: in the thick of battle,*
> *If my need be great enough*
> *It will blunt the edges of enemy swords,*
> *Their weapons will make no wounds.*

# Making your own Runes

### Why should you make your own Runes?

When you make your own set of Runes, you inject your own personal energy into them, and fill them with a power that will help you in your readings. A handmade set of Runes is a sign of your dedication to the craft, and these will mean much more to you than a set purchased in a shop. Making a set of Runes need not be difficult.

You may wish to learn the meanings of the Runes before you begin to make your set, although the act of making the Runes is itself an aid to this. It is best to start by learning the symbols and drawing them on a piece of paper until they become familiar.

A set of Runes that you have made for yourself is so highly personal that you will not want anyone else to handle them. You may also consider making a bag or box to keep them in. Natural fibers such as silk or linen are normally used for such bags, which can then be embroidered with one or more Rune designs. The bag will need to be large enough to hold all your Runes and to allow your hand to slip into it in order to pull the Runes out. You may choose to keep the bag inside a special box or inside a second bag made of a tougher material, such as leather.

## Choosing your material

Runes have traditionally been made from a variety of materials, though many modern sets are made from wood. Anything robust and lasting is suitable as Runes are bound to receive a lot of wear and tear. Each type of material has its unique energy and history.

You may wish to gather and use stones, or cut small slices from a fallen tree branch. You can use clay or some other material…the possibilities are endless. Using stones or gemstones will give you a durable and lasting set, but you will need to ensure that you have enough stones of the same size and texture, because you should not be able to tell which Rune is which, simply by touch. Wood can be cut, sanded and painted, but wood burns easily, holds water well and is difficult to clean. So it may not be the best choice for you unless you varnish your Runes. Some people find that varnishing their Runes gives them an artificial feel.

In the long run you may want to make a variety of sets to use for different purposes or to suit your mood. Excellent sets of Runes can be made from evenly shaped stones, ceramic tiles, wooden sticks and self-hardening clay. Once they are painted or engraved with the appropriate Rune symbol they become far more powerful than any you can buy in a shop.

Some purists even disapprove of buying raw materials to make Runes rather than going out and finding them oneself, but it is the finished Runes that need to be personal rather than the materials they are made from or the place where these were obtained. It is not particularly easy for someone who lives in the center of a modern city to pick up pebbles or slice a limb from a tree, so a little common sense should be allowed to prevail here.

## Script

Whatever material you use, you need to decide exactly what script you are going to use for your Runes. The Elder Futhark is the oldest, simplest and has the most written about it, and is the one that I have used in this book. If you decide to make additional sets in the future you can use alternative scripts for different sets.

## Stones

There are many choices when it comes to gathering stones to make Runes. The stones themselves need not be special, but you may choose to gather them from a place that has meaning for you – maybe from your own garden. The stones you gather will need to be as similar in weight and size as possible. They need to be thoroughly washed to remove dirt, dust and grime. You can then varnish the stones before painting a symbol on each or you could paint directly onto the stones with acrylic paints and then varnish with an acrylic sealer. Acrylic is water-soluble until dry, so it is easy to correct any mistakes you might make. The sealer will ensure that the paint does not get chipped when the Runes rub together in your bag. If you choose a glossy varnish, this will make them look shiny.

If you are skilled in carving, you could carve the Runes into the stones. Miniature chisels, files or a modeling drill with an engraving bit can be used. You will need a clamp or vise to hold the stones while you work on them.

If you are considering a trip to the West Country or to Wales, take a walk along the beaches. There you will be able to pick up wonderful flat red and gray slate or slate-like stones that have natural sheen and which look like coins. You can then paint these with acrylic paints.

## Wood

Runic designs were first carved into wood, which is why they are formed from lines rather than bends, curves or circles. The way to do this is to cut across the grain of the wood rather than going with the grain, which will make the designs appear to vanish into the wood's growth rings. One simple way to make wooden Runes is to use oval discs bought from a craft shop.

Birch, yew or fruit trees are often used for making Runes while fruit-bearing trees are more traditional - but you can choose any tree that appeals to you. Always make an offering to the tree before you cut into it and tell it why you want to take its wood. You might want to cut a branch bending to the North, or perhaps some other direction that appeals to you. Many people prefer to search for fallen branches than cutting into living wood but ensure that this is not so dried out that the surface of the Runes is likely to be rough. If you do cut into living wood, you will need to thank the tree for the gift that it has given you. The branch can then be cut into circular discs and the Runes can then be marked by pencil, and finally painted, carved, engraved, inked or burned into the wood. It takes about 30 inches of branch to make a full Rune set plus a few blanks for spares in case one or two get damaged later. Once you cut or marked the Runes onto the wood, you can add a decorative color or stain to the design. Each set made in this way will be unique, bearing the characteristics of a single branch from a single tree. A gloss finish is most attractive for the majority of woods, but Ash, Rowan, Sycamore and a few others look better with a mat surface.

Yew has a long history of association with the Runes and with magic, but there are many other woods that have their own magical associations. Rune spells and talismans were traditionally cut or scratched into the type of wood that was appropriate for a specific type of spell or energy.

Certain trees have long held a special significance as both practical providers and powerful spiritual forces. The specific trees varied in different areas, but those that were held to be sacred shared much in common. A tree of unusual size or beauty, or the wide range of materials it provided or a unique physical characteristic might set it apart and make it especially suitable. Sometimes simply the power of the tree's spirit could grant it a central place in the folklore and mythology of a culture - and even in these modern times, certain trees capture our imagination. The list below shows the types of tree and their associated gods and ideas.

## Trees and their Ancient Associations

*Alder*

This tree has an oily, water resistant wood and is used for making whistles. It is associated with one of the Giants who later became part of Welsh Celtic mythology as "Bran the Blest" who legend has it, brought the cross to Britain. It is said that his head is buried under the White Tower at the Tower of London. This tree is said to endow the person who uses it as an amulet protection and oracular powers.

*Apple*

This tree has a dense, fine-grained, rosy-colored wood with a slightly sweet smell. In Norse myth, Idhunna was the keeper of the "apples of immortality" which kept the Gods young. It is associated with choice and is useful for love and healing.

*Ash*

This tree has a strong, straight-grained wood. The European variety was referred to in the Eddas as the species of Yggdrasil - the "World-Tree". Ash can be used in spells requiring focus and strength of purpose, and is concerned with linking the inner and outer worlds.

*Beech*

This tree has a closely grained wood. Beech is concerned with ancient knowledge as revealed in old objects, places and writings. Beech indicates guidance from the past, and for the purpose of gaining the kind of insight that protects. Beech provides a solid base upon which all relies.

*Birch*

This tree has a pale, fine-grained wood. It is associated with fertility and healing magic. Within living memory, criminals in British prisons were at actually "birched" (hit with a collection of birch sticks) as a punishment. One wonders whether the worthies who did this realized that they were following a pagan tradition that was designed to drive out the evil influences that had supposedly entered the criminal that they thrashed! Birch was associated with Thor and it is a useful adjunct for fertility and healing spells.

### Blackthorn

A winter tree, Blackthorn has a black bark and is covered with vicious thorns and it grows in dense thickets. The wood is used for making the cudgel and shillelagh. Its thorns were used to pierce waxen images. Blackthorn indicates the irresistible action of fate or outside influences that must be obeyed.

### Elder

In Norse mythology, the Goddess Freya chose the black elder for her home. In medieval times it was the abode of witches and it was considered dangerous to sleep under its branches or to cut it down. Elder indicates the end in the beginning, and the beginning in the end.

### Elm

The elm tree has a slightly fibrous, tan-colored wood with a slight sheen. Elm is associated with the mother and earth goddesses and it said to be the abode of "faeries". Elm wood is valued for its resistance to splitting. The inner bark was used for cordage and chair caning. Elm adds stability and grounding to a spell.

### Fir

Fir cones respond to rain by closing and to the sun by opening. Fir is said to be able to see over great distance to the far horizon beyond and below. It indicates high views and long sight with clear vision of what is beyond and yet to come.

### Hawthorn

This tree has a light, hard, apple-like wood. The wood from the hawthorn provides the hottest fire known. In medieval Europe it was associated with witchcraft and considered to be unlucky. Hawthorn can be used for protection, love and marriage spells.

### Hazel

Hazel is commonly used for water divining. Magically, hazel wood is used to gain knowledge, wisdom and poetic inspiration.

### Holly

This tree has a beautiful white wood with an almost invisible grain. Holly is associated with the symbolism of the death of the land in winter and its rebirth in spring in both Pagan and Christian lore. Holly may be used in spells for sleep or rest and also to ease the passage of death.

### Larch

This tree has a light, soft wood, which is very similar to that of spruce. The smoke from burning larch is said to ward off evil spirits. Larch may be used for protection and to induce visions.

### Maple

This tree has a very hard, pale, fine-grained wood. Maple can bring success and abundance.

### Oak

This tree has a richly colored dark brown wood. Oak has been considered sacred by just about every culture that has encountered the tree, although it was held in particular esteem by the Norse and Celts because of its size, longevity and its nutritious acorns. The oak is frequently associated with Thor. Oak can be used in spells for protection, strength, success and stability.

### Pine

This tree is an evergreen and it is associated with guilt or feelings of guilt.

### Poplar

The Anglo-Saxon Rune poem to refers to the poplar as being associated with the Rune Berkano. The poplar is associated with the ability to resist and to shield, to endure and conquer. A further association links this tree with speech, language and also with the winds.

*Rowan*

The rowan tree is long known for its ability to protect against enchantment, and it indicates protection and control of the senses from enchantment, seduction and beguiling.

*Willow*

The willow is a water-loving tree. In western tradition it is a symbol of mourning and unlucky love. Willow indicates cycles, rhythms and the ebb and flux of events and of life.

*Yew*

This tree has a smooth, gold-colored wood with a wavy grain. Long associated with magic, death, rebirth - and the Runes. The yew is said be the oldest-lived tree in the world, although this belief arose before the discovery of Australia and the much older forms of antipodean tree. There are convincing arguments for it being the original "World Tree" of Scandinavian mythology. Yew may be used to enhance magical and psychic abilities and to induce visions.

*Bone*

Another natural product that may be used for Runes is horn or bone. Some people have been known to collect the bones after a barbecue for this purpose! If you want to use bones you need to boil them for several hours until all the meat and marrow are gone and they are bleached white. To cut the tiles you will need a hacksaw and blade that is capable of cutting through bone. After painting the symbols you will need to seal the bone so that the paint does not chip off. Bone can become very brittle, so it needs to be coated with varnish.

### Clay

Traditional clay can be used to make Runes but it will need to be fired, so it is of most use to those of you who are in contact with people who make and fire pottery. Having said this, it is now possible to buy clay that will dry in the air or that can be dried in an oven. This is the easiest of all the products mentioned in this chapter to obtain as it is available in all those places where toys and games are sold. You can form the clay into small balls and then flatten these slightly against a table so that you can use a sharp stick or a knife to incise the Runes on the stones. When hardened, the marks can be made to stand out by filling in the incisions and then varnishing the tablets. The pieces can also be stained before painting. Clay is available in numerous colors so it is easy to choose one that reflects the nature of each of your Runes.

### Other materials

The glass stones that are sold to be put into the bottom of fish tanks come in a variety of colors, and these can be painted with enamel paints or engraved or scratched. Ice lolly sticks can be collected and painted, as can seashells, card or pieces of leather. Traditional Runes are made from bone or wood, because these were the materials most readily available in the past, but modern possibilities are endless, and they need not cost much money. One of the pleasures of casting Runes is the tactile sensation they offer, so the choice of your material should be based on the feel and weight that you find most appealing.

### Marking the Runes

Traditionally, blood would often be used to mark a set of Runes, so traditionalists still choose a red colored medium for this, but it is not essential. Your choice of method will depend very much on the material that you have chosen to fabricate your Runes from. If you are painting onto a flat surface, then acrylic or enamel paints which available from most craft and hobby shops will be suitable. You will need a good quality, fine paintbrush for your work. If you are using wood, the Runes can be burnt onto your slices with a tool designed for the purpose or by applying a heated metal skewer. If you have incised your Runes then you may want to rub a metallic paint into your slices in order to highlight the script.

### Consecrating your Runes

Once you have finished making your set of Runes you should consecrate them. Consecration is an act that implies making something special, and it also incorporates a principle of cleansing. The firsts stage of consecration is called smudging, which means exposing the Runes to the smoke of herbs or incense. This stage takes the Runes through Air, representing the mind, and then smoke, representing the spirit. The second stage uses salt sprinkled over the Runes, which is symbolic of the earth. Rather than applying salt, some people bury their Runes in the earth for a few days. The third stage is water, so some spring water should be poured into a clean dish and the Runes submerged in it. The fourth stage of consecration is through fire. This can be done by swiftly passing each Rune through the flame of a burning candle.

After the Runes have been consecrated they can be activated for use. This can be done by placing each Rune in the palm of your left hand, making a cylinder of your hand and then blowing through it. These Runes are now personal to you alone, and they should not be used by other people - except perhaps in an emergency and only with your express permission. While you are consecrating your Runes, you may want to consider each Rune, meditate on its meaning and also ask Odin to bless them for you.

# Interpreting the Aettir

There are three Aettir (Aettir is the plural of Aett) in the Elder Futhark, and they form a careful division of the Runes. One of their functions is to act as part of an initiatory structure, each Aett being one degree in a three-degree initiation system. Initiation systems are a method of moving from one level of competence, knowledge or skill to the next. If we took the army as an example, a soldier would start out as a Private, be promoted to Corporal and then Sergeant. In astrology, a person would start by learning how to interpret a natal chart, then add predictive techniques and so on, increasing his standard of knowledge and skill as he went. The same idea exists in the study and application of magic, the qabala, freemasonry, religion or any other system that has a recognized promotion ladder that is based on knowledge and skill. The Aettir also reflect the ancient society division of nurturer, warrior and priest/king. The divisions are reflected in the Aettir of the Runes in different ways. There is overlap in the duties of the Runes and each Aett has its compliment of functions and its own character.

Each Aett ends with a Rune of positive nature and successively greater scope. Each contains certain Runes that - directly or indirectly - cover similar concepts. For example each has a Rune for light. (Kanauz the torch,

Sowelo the sun and Dagaz the day.) The light becomes greater in power as we progress through the Aettir. Similarly, each also has a Rune referring to wealth (Fehu, Nauthiz and Othila).

Each of Aettir has a different emphasis. Freya has four Runes of danger, evil or cost (Uruz, Thurisaz, Raido and Gebo). Hagal has three (Nauthiz, Isa and Pertho) and Tiwaz only one (Laguz, the dangerous sea). Each has at least one Rune of protection, one that is useful as a good luck charm and one that is used in healing magic. The structure of the Aettir makes it probable that the Runes were probably taught in groups of three. The declining number of negative Runes and the increase in complexity as one progresses through them emphasizes the suggestion that they were taught as a degree system. Each Aett has its own major concerns. Freya's is concerned with love, happiness and enjoyment, Hagal's with matters of achievement, power and success, and Tyr's with justice, order and spiritual advancement. In other words, the Runes progress through from personal and emotional concerns of love and pleasure, through worldly concerns of battle and achievement to spiritual concerns of justice and godliness.

The next section examines the meanings of the individual Runes. The interpretations are divided into the three Aettir. Some people choose to give different meanings to a Rune that falls in a reversed position. However, not all of the Runes can be read in the reversed position, so some other Rune users maintain that, although each Rune may contain a negative form, its positive or negative energy is derived from its position amongst surrounding Runes. In the following section the meanings are given for the negative form of each Rune, and I leave it up to you whether you chose to read reversed Runes differently or not. Alternative names commonly given to the Runes are also outlined.

### The Blank Rune

It is not traditional to use a blank Rune although many commercially produced sets do include one. If you decide to include this in your set, you can consider its appearance as a kind of fated event, or something that is beyond the questioner's control for good or ill. The closest approximation to this is the Wheel of Fortune in the Tarot, which simply indicates that some kind of change is about to take place, but whether this is for good or ill depends upon the rest of the reading. In the case of the Runes, the feeling is that fate, destiny, karma or the uncontrollable force of Wyrd, (the goddess of praise and punishment), is at hand - for good or ill.

## Freya's Aett
*Fehu, Uruz, Thurisaz, Ansuz, Raido, Kaunuz, Gebo, Wunjo.*

**FEHU**

### One
### Fehu
*Feh, fe, faihu, feoh. The sound of "f"*
**Origin**

The root meaning of the Fehu Rune is cattle. Cattle were an important aspect of the life of any agricultural community and they were vital to the economy. Therefore, this Rune represents possessions won or earned and points achieved on the road to material gain. In the Anglo-Saxon runic poem, wealth is described as a "comfort to all men", and the poem goes on to say that it must be bestowed freely for those who wish to gain favor. In the Icelandic Rune poem, wealth is regarded as a source of discord. Generally linked to the Aesir, this Rune is also often linked to Freya as it is first in Freya's Aett.

**Positive interpretation**

Fehu is concerned with wealth, material fulfillment and ownership, and in modern terms, this includes money. In general it represents happiness and prosperity but it also represents the kind of property that can be sold and bought. It indicates success in ventures, as it represents not only the power to obtain wealth, but also the strength needed to hold on to it, thus Fehu is also a Rune of power and control.

This being the first Rune in the set, one would suppose that it suggests a time of beginnings, of fresh starts, but in many ways this refers to the previous phase and cycles that have already been completed. It shows that you have reached your goals, accomplished what you are trying to achieve and that it is time to rest and enjoy the fruits of your labors. The loose ends have been tied up, you have gained abundance through your efforts and you now have a kind of inheritance of well-deserved self-esteem, self-value and success in ventures past.

Furthermore, there is a hint of further success to come. Fehu announces the arrival of the things that you have worked for, and it also suggests that you will overcome future opposition. It advises you to stick with whatever plan you have underway, and sometimes also to conserve and hold onto what you have.

Fehu is concerned with your physical and financial needs and the self-esteem that can be gained from meeting these. It speaks of enjoying good fortune through sharing it with others. In modern terms, Fehu represents earned income, so it is relates to your career, status and position in the world. When appearing in a casting it can indicate that prosperity is coming to you in some form, perhaps financially. The precise type of gain will be indicated by the Runes that surround it. For example, if it is with Berkano it shows gain as a result of a personal relationship.

The feeling is that a successful cycle has been completed and that it is now time to take the next step.

### Negative or reversed interpretation

When reversed or surrounded by negative Runes, Fehu may indicate a lack of wealth and a period of financial difficulty. It may also be interpreted as greed and an exaggerated interest in material matters. Fehu can indicate loose ends and unfinished projects. In its most negative form, Fehu represents loss, or possibly an offer that should not be accepted.

It is connected to poverty and also the kind of domination by others that leads to a loss of self-esteem. If not strongly negative it can indicate a delay or obstacle. Fehu may caution you to avoid wasting resources and to think carefully of the effect your actions will have in the future.

In some cases, this can indicate problems related to conception, fertility and pregnancy.

### Magical uses

In magic, Fehu is used to attract wealth and to protect property, as well as to gain power over the environment. As an amulet, it can be used for protection and to increase your power.

URUZ

## Two
## Uruz
## Ur. The sound of "oo"

### Origin

Uruz represents the aurochs, the once great wild cattle of northern Europe that could never be tamed and which are now extinct. Julius Caesar described them in "De Bello Gallico" as slightly less than the elephant in size and of the color and shape of a bull. They had extraordinary strength and speed and were exceptionally ferocious. They were seen as a symbol of great strength and speed as well as a symbol of man's prowess. It is believed that the bull was dedicated to Thor, so this Rune is often associated with him. Hunting the aurochs provided a test of strength and initiative, so this is seen as a Rune of achievement. Uruz is also often taken to represent Urd, who is the crone-like eldest of the three Norns.

Uruz is associated with the old gods – the Vanir. It represents the primal creative force, so it represents assertive action, a bid for liberty or a force that is contained straining to be free. It can denote a protective force, especially in reference to your children or your territory. In general terms, Uruz represents a formative or protective force that can shape things to come.

### Positive interpretation

Uruz is always concerned with some sort of beginning, the birth of something new and the end of one cycle and the start of another. It represents challenges and everything concerning the unknown. This Rune contains great creative power, it also represents free will and the ability to make decisions that can take you onwards into new circumstances. It is a force for change and shows a time to take action. Personal success could be at hand, and you need to be ready to accept the power that comes with it. Uruz is the Rune of strength, good health and sometimes also advancement in your career. When included in a casting it can show that your dream or wish is coming to pass. In some positions it can represent the male in a relationship. Uruz represents a strong, masculine force of energy and assertiveness.

The appearance of Uruz suggests that you will soon notice an improvement in business and finances, although you have to work for these. Although there are new challenges are ahead, you will have the energy to work at them. It is primarily a Rune of good fortune, exciting events and success. Uruz represents energy, passion, vitality, fertility and the unconscious. It is mostly concerned with the natural and instinctive sides of our nature. It also represents bravery, questing, initiation, challenge, untamed spirit, masculinity, stamina, independence, strength and action. The outlook is particularly good for vitality and the return of health after a period of sickness.

*Negative or reversed interpretation*

In its negative form Uruz represents brutality, harshness, hatred and change for the worse, also possibly having your own power used against you. It can indicate an unwillingness to take chances or to approach the unknown. It symbolizes a lack of will-power and motivation. Uruz is also connected with male violence, callousness and abuse. When Uruz is included in a reading it can indicate that you have failed to take advantage of the moment, and that it may be your own low self-image that is holding you back. As this Rune also represents low vitality, it can occasionally be indicative of sexual problems for a man. It can be seen as unlucky and indicates that a lack of energy or motivation may be the reason for missing out on opportunities to improve your life or your circumstances.

### Magical uses

In magic, Uruz is used to clear obstacles or change circumstances. As an amulet, it can be used to galvanize the wearer into action or to increase sexual potency.

**THURISAZ**

## Three
### *Thurisaz*
*Thurisars, Thurs, thauris, thyth, thurisa. The sound of "th" as in "thin"*

### *Origin*

Although the precise meaning of this Rune has been disputed, it is generally accepted as being unpleasant in nature. It is usually taken to mean "thorn" and it is associated with giants, trolls and demons. When used in a sequence of three Runes, it can alter the meanings of succeeding two Runes. It is said to have been used to invoke demons from the underworld. The meaning of thorn symbolizes a sharp and unpleasant thing to touch - and it may also have sexual connotations.

Thurisaz is a Rune of the force that can be used for defense or for destruction. Thorny bushes were once used to protect boundaries and to enclose criminals. Thor is the god that is said to protects sacred enclosures, so this Rune is associated with him. It is also associated with the Thursur, who were giants in Norse mythology. These are primal forces, elemental in nature. Therefore, this is a Rune of testing and challenge as well as protection and defense.

### *Positive interpretation*

This Rune represents chaos and transformation, the destruction that is needed to allow space for renewal. It is also connected with lust and the combination of pleasure and pain. It can be frightening due to its habit of revealing our darkest and most destructive natures. The fact is that we have to tear down the old to make room for the new, so this Rune represents a type of catharsis from which new energy and insight may arise.

Thurisaz opens the door to the future. It shows the survival of difficulties and the need to do the right thing, to take the right action and to resist oppression or opposition. At times it indicates a sudden change without warning. It is associated with stubbornness and perhaps the need to put one's own entrenched opinions aside listen to advice. It is also a Rune of protection, symbolizing passive resistance and the ability to attack without fighting, and thus it can outlast disorder and chaos. Being associated with boundaries and the kind of thorny hedges that are used to keep cattle from straying, it signifies that you should understand your limitations and calculate any risky ventures with care. Challenges will be fraught with danger and there is even a risk of injury, so care must be taken.

When in a positive combination, protection and luck are at your side. However it falls, Thurisaz indicates that an important decision is at hand, and this can be of such vital importance that it may change your life forever. Reflection, due consideration and seeking out good advice is essential if you want to take the right decision. Although hardship may be present, there should also be wisdom, because this Rune demands a sense of focus and deep introspection.

*Negative or reversed interpretation*

In its negative form, Thurisaz represents an unwillingness to listen to information and advice, and the kind of obstinacy that can lead to conflict. A cycle of good luck may come to an end, so this is not the time to boast or to be too self-assured. There may be opposition that comes from those who are stronger than you. It gives a warning to be cautious in making decisions and to slow down, check out possibilities and see what can be done. In short, if you proceed now, you must do so with immense caution - but if you are unsure of the outcome of a specific decision or action, perhaps it is best to do nothing for the time being.

### Magical uses

In magic, Thurisaz is used for protection and defense or for those occasions when one needs to strike back at others. As an amulet it can be worn for protection.

ANSUZ

## Four
### Ansuz
*Ass, ansus, ansur, os. The sound of "ah"*
**Origin**

This Rune has the meaning of a god, or deity - specifically one of the Aesir and it is usually ascribed to Odin. It is related to the story of Odin and the way that he obtained the knowledge of the Runes, so Ansuz is associated with the source of all language. It is also considered to be a blessing, joy and comfort for the wise. As the worldly counterpart of the world-tree Yggdrasil, the ash tree is associated with this Rune and this reinforces the connection with Odin.

This is the Rune of inspired speech and incantation as a form of creative expression. It is linked with the passing of knowledge through the spoken word, and by extension it is also considered to be the Rune of the poet. It represents the acquisition of inspiration and understanding. Ansuz is also associated with enthusiasm, manipulation, encouragement and compassion. As the Rune of the gods Ansuz is very powerful, as it represents divine powers and the intervention of the gods. It denotes all forms of direct communication, such as speaking and singing, and suggests that a combination of these can lead to divine inspiration, spiritual insight and wisdom.

*Positive interpretation*

Ansuz symbolizes honesty, inspiration and the good use of words, and it also advises you to listen to your own inner voice. All matters related to communication are covered by this Rune, including news, study and teaching. Ansuz represents wisdom, sometimes the kind that emanates from the most unlikely source. It is the Rune of intellectual activities and also of stability and order. As it represents the spoken word and communication, Ansuz is associated with taking advice and the acquisition of wisdom. In a reading it often represents an intelligent individual who is full of energy. It can show someone wiser (and perhaps older) than yourself who is able to offer good advice. Sometimes Ansuz suggests an apprenticeship under the guidance of someone who is able to teach you a great deal. It can also indicate a verbal test such as an oral exam or a job interview, and in this circumstance Ansuz will show that you can get through the test with ease. It indicates that knowledge may come from the most unexpected of sources and it also suggests that a little positive trickery can be helpful in the current circumstances. Sometimes this shows that whatever has been holding you back will shortly remove itself.

*Negative or reversed interpretation*

In its negative form Ansuz refers to dishonesty, lies, trickery and a refusal to learn the lessons of life. It shows loss and misunderstandings as well as betrayal. Others may interfere with your plans or there could be a breakdown in communication. The advice you receive could be biased, thus it would be a good idea to seek a second opinion. Things are unclear and knowledge may be being misused in some way. Sometimes it indicates an elderly person who is causing problems. In practical terms, this denotes a phase when letters go missing, communications become fouled up and journeys that should be straightforward turn into nightmares.

### Magical uses

In magic, Ansuz is used to bring calm and for help in making wise decisions, and also as a general aid in divination. As an amulet it can be worn to increase communication skills.

RAIDO

# Five
## Raido
**Reid, rad, raidho, raida, reda. The sound of "r"**
### Origin

Many meanings have been ascribed to this Rune; a journey, a cartwheel, a ride and a cart. It is often associated with Thor, who rode in a wheeled chariot, and thus also to thunder, which tradition tells us was caused when Thor drove his chariot across the sky. It is also associated with the god Foresti, the god of justice and son of Baldur.

Usually Raido is associated with wagons, which make it the Rune of the traveler, and it can offer protection to the traveler. As Raido also signifies the passage of the sun and stars through the heavens, it is also associated with spiritual and mental journeys and can indicate that there is a path to follow that can solve a particular problem.

### Positive interpretation

Raido refers to travel and also the means of transportation. It may signify a journey that is taken by necessity or one that is taken for pleasure, and if this is a literal journey, it will be safe, pleasant and enjoyable. However, Raido can show a metaphorical pathway or road, which can be a way through a dilemma, a journey in consciousness or a change of view. It represents the "vehicle" or method by which you achieve an object or goal. It allows you to channel your energies effectively so that they will help you. Thus, the journey in question may be a journey of the soul, taken in order to bring about some form of healing. Representing movement and motion, Raido symbolizes travel and exploration, but it can also denote a new start, taking control, leadership and promotions. This Rune suggests that this is a good time for negotiations and discussions and a time when it is possible to reach a compromise. Depending on the surrounding Runes it may indicate unexpected news or that this is a good time to buy or sell something of importance. In modern terms, this might be a vehicle, a computer, fax, telephone or some other form of communications equipment. Raido can refer to a quest and your destiny in following such a quest. Decisions need to be made alongside an ability to see the larger picture, as it advises not to focus solely on your problems or become isolated from daily events but to take the wider view.

### Negative or reversed interpretation

In its negative form, Raido suggests that this is a bad time for traveling, despite the fact you may need to do so. Delays, accidents, breakdowns and problems are likely in any journey that you must take. Plans are likely to be upset, so it is best to postpone your journey for the time being if at all possible. It can indicate an unexpected and unplanned journey. Sometimes this refers to a course of action is best left for the time being. Negotiations are unlikely to turn out well at this time and you may have to be extra patient with people. It is best to avoid legal or official dealings for the time being. It may signify a lack of goals and stagnation in your life and the need to stop, think and see what lessons need to be learned.

### Magical uses

In magic, Raido is used to help you when searching into the unknown and to help you to take control. As an amulet it can be worn to ensure a safe journey and to aid you in legal matters.

**KAUNAZ**

## Six
### *Kaunaz*
*Kano, ken, kenaz, kauna, cen, kusma, chosma. The sound of "k"*

**Origin**

A variety of meanings have been attributed to this Rune including a torch or light, a boil, abscess and an ulcer. The most common attribution is "torch" although several sources do associate it with some form of discomfort or disease. It is also associated with cremation. Kaunaz represents internal fire on all levels, including that of inflammation and fever. This is the flame of the forge and deep earth energies, so it has an association with the Dwarves who dwell in the deep earth. It is the flame of the artist and craftsman and therefore, a force for creation, and there is a close association with knowledge that is derived from such inspiration. At times it represents the fire of a sexual relationship or the barrier that needs to be crossed in order to reach inner knowledge.

**Positive interpretation**

Primarily, Kaunaz is concerned with illumination and also the destruction needed in order to make way for the new. It is concerned with dangerous forces that are hard to control. Although these forces are needed for our survival they can also easily harm us. It denotes insight, learning and knowledge, wisdom and enlightenment. When you are in the dark, this Rune offers an opportunity to realize your highest potential. It can lead to new beginnings, but it can also represent the light of guidance and learning, because the light that it shines brings clarity and revelation.

Kaunaz is a Rune of spiritual as well as intellectual enlightenment. It may also indicate good health and a positive attitude. If your life has been stagnating, this Rune can show a change for the better. It is a good Rune to find if you are undertaking any creative activity. Kaunaz suggests that the solution to your problems will be forthcoming, also that this is a time for seriousness and concentration. Sometimes Kaunaz represents a form of intellectual passion, but it can also occasionally denote physical and sexual passion. Whatever the scene, Kaunaz brings heightened emotions.

### *Negative or reversed interpretation*

In its negative form, Kaunaz depicts a darkening of the light and perhaps a missed opportunity. It signifies the loss of illusion and false hope. It can represent an ending or loss, and sometimes also poor judgment on your part. Often it shows up when a personal relationship is coming to a permanent end. The lack of clarity associated with this Rune leads to confusion and disillusionment.

### *Magical uses*

In magic, it is used to restore self-confidence and strengthen willpower. As an amulet it can be worn to enhance your insight.

GEBO

## Seven
### Gebo
*Gifu, gebu, giba, gewa, gifu, gyfu. The sound of "g"*
### Origin
This Rune means a gift, although the nature of the gift remains ambiguous. It is unclear whether it refers to the sacrifice of humanity to the gods or the bounty of the gods to man. It is often translated to mean generosity. Gebo is often associated with Odin or Freya. As the gift Rune, Gebo is concerned with mutual and unselfish giving. It represents the ability to sacrifice without expecting anything in return. Gebo also symbolizes the connection between the gods and men. It is the gift that brings connections through exchange, and it signifies the unity and honor created when an exchange takes place.

### Positive interpretation
Gebo represents hospitality, generosity and giving. It is the point where the giver joins the one who receives. It has been related to the gift of wisdom received by the hero from the Valkyries. As a symbol of exchanged vows, marriage and ecstasy it also represents sacrifice of independence due to partnership, but also increase due to consolidation. Joint efforts, partnership, love and growth are represented by this Rune. It is associated with all matters related to sharing and sacrifice. Often it will signify a new romance or an important development in a romantic relationship because Gebo suggests commitment. The gift it represents may be one of love or a material one

that comes along just when you need it. It tells of a gift that binds a partnership. It usually indicates a time in your life that is full of peace and contentment.

Gebo can refer to an unexpected gain and benefits that arise from a joint effort. The relationship it refers to may the one that we have with our higher selves, and the sense of unity with all that surrounds us. Generally thought of as being lucky, Gebo shows the creation of harmony within relationships and the ability to balance opposing forces.

*NB:* It is common for us to sign the letters and cards that we send to our loved ones with an "X", but how many of us realize that we are actually using the Gebo Rune for this purpose?

### Negative or reversed interpretation

Although Gebo is one of the Runes that cannot be read in its reversed position, depending on the surrounding Runes it may still have a negative form. It can indicate dishonesty, a lack of balance or problems that are rooted in your emotions. Another thing to bear in mind is that if you are too ready to give to others, they may become reliant on your generosity rather than standing on their own feet. In addition, if you stop giving or if you do not give enough in a particular situation, you may be seen as a miser.

### Magical uses

In magic, Gebo is used to promote harmony and bring about union as well as to receive divine instruction. As an amulet it may be worn to bring harmony into your romantic life.

WUNJO

# Eight
## Wunjo
*Wynja, wunju, winne, vend, wyn. The sound of "v" or "w"*

### Origin

This Rune means bliss, comfort and glory and it primarily represents an absence of suffering. It is also associated with intoxication. It is one of the two Runes that represent joy, (the other being Sowelo). Wunjo represents physical and sensual energy and it carries a sense of playfulness with it. It is connected to the god Freyr due to its meaning of peace and joy. Love and falling in love are typical aspects of this Rune. It is very much concerned with living in the present and indicates a condition of physical and emotional well-being.

### Positive interpretation

Wunjo is associated with happiness and joy and the battle that is well-fought and won. It offers prosperity and friendship. Being associated with the wind, Wunjo can also be the means by which you alter the direction of something or change one situation into another – or perhaps run against the wind. It represents a state of harmony in a chaotic world and it provides a balance between all things. It shows the meeting point between opposites and the point at which alienation disappears. This is a Rune of shared aims and it can mean that good news will come from afar.

Often Wunjo indicates luck, happiness and success coming into your life. It may show deep affection and lasting emotional happiness. If may represent a person in a reading, especially when this person is the object of your affections. Sometimes this indicates a firm friendship rather than love. In general it represents pleasure and bliss, peace and serenity, along with a sense of fulfillment and harmony, and of hopes and wishes coming true. It rules the virtue of cheerfulness and suggests that you are able to keep any pain and sorrow from looming too large in your life. Wunjo indicates recognition of your achievements and the reward for your efforts. It can offer relief after a time of strife and it indicates that life is making a turn for the better. Sometimes this Rune indicates good news from afar and also the return of health after a period of sickness, especially if there is someone around who helps you get back on your feet.

### Negative or reversed interpretation

In its negative form Wunjo represents impractical enthusiasm and unrealistic expectations, and it suggests unhappiness and sadness. Matters involving trust are at issue now and it may be that someone you love and trust or rely upon in business is turning out to be untrustworthy. At times it can show failure and loneliness. It may describe dissatisfaction with your job or performance. It suggests that you need to be cautious and put off important decisions. Trouble may be coming from people who oppose you, but this will soon pass. Tradition says that you should delay decisions of a personal nature for at least three months, or of a business nature for at least three days.

### Magical uses

In magic, Wunjo is used to bring happiness and success. As an amulet it can be worn to bring success to all your endeavors.

# Hagal's Aett

*Hagalaz, Nauthiz, Isa, Jera, Eihwaz, Pertho, Algiz, Sowelo.*

**HAGALAZ**

### Nine
*Hagalaz*
*Hagal, hagl, haal, hagel, haegl. The sound of "h"*
*Origin*

The meaning of this Rune is hail. This Rune recognizes the potential for destruction and qualities of transformation. It is as though a period of frost and snow is required in order to break up and refresh the earth so that it can bring forth new fertility and growth. Representing primal chaos, it is associated with Ymir. Out of this chaos comes a tangible force, which means that Hagalaz signifies a dramatic event or disruption to one's life that comes from outside, and possibly from a completely unexpected source. A hailstorm can be devastating and it can ruin everything that lies in its path. Hagalaz is one of three Runes associated with winter, which to people living in the ancient Norse lands of Sweden and Norway, means a period of bad weather, wind, snow, ice and restriction. The Norsemen were great travelers, so a bad winter made travel difficult, if not downright impossible. In time all things can transform from something bad to something good. This is a Rune of the unconscious mind and the thought process. It rules the laws that shape events in our lives, which suggests that the force it represents is not completely under our control.

### Positive interpretation

Hagalaz foretells a time of utter destruction of all that is familiar to you and the kind of major event occurs in every life once in a while. Such a scenario might be a death in the family, divorce, sickness, sudden financial loss or some other form of major setback. Sometimes it is merely a longed-for journey that has to be set aside. Fate is not with you at this time and life is hard - indeed, in some cases quite terrifying for a while.

However, Hagalaz is not simply destructive, it offers opportunity for great change and perhaps a journey from one world or lifestyle to another. It represents forces that cannot be avoided. As the Rune of unexpected disruptions, it also signifies limitations and delays. The forces at work here are outside your control, and it may only be later you that you will see a reason for the limitations that are being imposed on you or the risks that you are being forced to take. Hagalaz refers to a time of testing, trial, penance, loss, pain and suffering. This demands that you let go of the past so that you have room for growth, acceptance and fortitude. Its influence is disruptive, but it allows you the freedom to break out of your current cycle. Even if you are afraid of change or refuse to leave the past behind, Hagalaz will force you to break out. This is not a time for long term plans as they are likely to be unsuccessful. Eventual success can be obtained but only after much effort on your part. When you look back on this time, it will stick in your mind as the time when your character was forged, when you developed a backbone and achieved or lived through more than you thought possible.

You may feel that your future is in the hands of another person and this may be someone who you are not particularly familiar with. The advice of this Rune is not to start anything new now. It can sometimes refer to an interruption rather than complete destruction. Oddly enough, because of its connection with risk, this is a Rune of gamblers and gambling.

### Negative or reversed interpretation

Hagalaz cannot be read reversed, but in its negative form shows chaos and disruption, loss and the need for shelter. It refers to unresolved matters, blaming others for shortcomings and nostalgia for what has gone before. This may indicate accidents that are caused by rash behavior or by moving to fast. This is not a time for taking risks or gambles, so stop and think before taking any important steps.

### Magical uses

In magic, it is used to remove unwanted influences and to break destructive patterns. As an amulet it can be worn to protect against external aggression.

NAUTHIZ

Ten
*Nauthiz*
*Naudhiz, naud, naurdirz, nied, nyd, naudhr, nauths.*
*The sound of "n"*

*Origin*

Nauthiz is another of the shaping powers that form the fates of the world and humanity. It is associated with the Nornir, who are the shapers. Nauthiz means "need", and is a Rune representing the desire that drives us to obtain that which we want. It is strongly associated with sexual desire in addition to the desire to obtain or achieve. When directed, it can be creative and procreative, but when misused, it can be a force for destruction.

*Positive interpretation*

This Rune's meaning vacillates between assistance and the need to survive. Working hard and making an effort will offer a solution to your difficulties at this time, although it can signal hardships and great challenges. Nauthiz encourages you to concentrate on the essentials, those things that really need to be done, rather than to procrastinate or concern yourself with trivialities. It may be interpreted as a power source, or perhaps as poverty and desperate need. Often it foretells hard work and a period of endurance. Necessity places constraints on you, so your possibilities are restricted, but it also brings the power and strength to break free from restriction. Often this Rune stands for delays and a need to exercise patience. It shows a time when you are passing through a difficult learning situation and a time when you are forced to face your fears. It is a time to avoid greed and to conserve your energy. Your emotional needs are unlikely to be met at this time. It is just possible that your problems are a result of blowing up a situation out of proportion.

Hardship, responsibility and discontent are symbolized by Nauthiz, along with the frustration that these lead to. It represents the desire for what you fancy or what you think you deserve versus real needs, and the endurance and patience that is needed to gain your desires. Nauthiz frequently indicates that you find yourself coming into contact with some part of yourself that you do not like. It shows a time to appreciate what you have, and to draw on your inner resources and strengths.

Assistance will come from older relatives and friends who stand by you through some very dark times. Determination and self-reliance can lead to change, but either way this Rune suggests that your luck will change for the better in the near future.

*Negative or reversed interpretation*

In its negative form, Nauthiz tells of a testing time when your patience and sanity are pushed to their limits. It advises you to avoid making hasty judgments or setting off on the wrong path, so it is important to realize your mistakes and to be honest with yourself. You may have to right wrongs you have done to others in the past. The advice here is to avoid get-rich-quick schemes or quick-fix solutions, but just to stick to the right path and wait for your luck to change.

*Magical uses*

In magic, Nauthiz is used to channel the kinetic energy that is tied up in sexual frustration and to give strength in times of need. As an amulet it can be worn to give inner strength in times of hardship.

ISA

## Eleven
### Isa
*Is, iss, isarz, eis, iiz. The sound of "i or ee"*
**Origin**

Isa means ice. Isa is an elemental Rune, associated with the Rind who refused Odin the means to avenge the death of his son. It is also associated with the Frost Giants who are called the Thursur. Like frozen water, ice is considered to be static, so can bring things to a halt. It may also be an expansive force, or one that crushes anything caught in its grasp. It may provide a bridge over dark water or a dangerous trap. Being self-contained it has the power of control and constraint.

Spontaneity and activity have no connection to Isa, as it emphasizes withdrawal and a time of standing still. There is an element of discipline contained in this Rune, enabling it to act as a very powerful force. It warns avoidance of any tendency to exaggerated formalism or inhibiting strictness. Monotony results from its more negative manifestation. It is an effective protection against vulnerability and it can hinder emotional involvement. Isa tends to halt activity and delay progress.

**Positive interpretation**

When Isa is drawn it indicates a time of standstill and a freeze in a situation, so all plans should be put on hold. It often indicates temporary delays and frustrations and it may also talk of a relationship that is cooling off. Bad feelings and resentments are possible, along with problems relating to loyalty. Where love relationships are concerned, this indicates a really painful time when you need to accept that your lover is losing interest and that you may have to call it a day and move on.

In one sense, the feeling of being frozen or in limbo can be a problem, but in another it also allows time for thought and a review of your situation. A sense of detachment comes about which enables you to focus your thoughts before moving onto a new stage. Reflection and withdrawal allow a time of rest and recuperation. It is time to shed outdated ideas so that you can unfreeze yourself from past patterns of behavior and to allow a thaw to follow. Just as spring follows winter, you will shortly turn the corner.

### Negative or reversed interpretation

Isa cannot be read in a reversed position, but in its negative form it shows cooling relationships, deceptive beauty, restrictions and delay. It shows the dangers of the path you are treading and the fact that you really do have to leave a no-win situation behind and move in a new direction.

### Magical uses

In magic, Isa is used to strengthen powers of concentration and stabilize the personality. It is not usually worn as an amulet.

JERA

## Twelve
## Jera
*Jara, jer, ger yer, ar. The sound of "y" as in "year"*
### Origin
The meanings attributed to this Rune include year, spear and harvest. It is connected with the completion of a cycle, the end of a season or the close of a year, so it represents the rotation and change of the cycles. It can represent fruitful completion or the eternal contrast of opposites that provide a whole. Jera can bring peace and harmony and it states that what was sown can be reaped.

The whole cycle of life is contained within this Rune of seed, growth and harvest. Jera represents the meeting between the seasons, between light and darkness, day and night, man and woman. It signifies the sacred marriage ritual between god and goddess. Its association with sex as a means of survival as well as enjoyment leads to Jera's association with Freya. It also represents hopes and expectations for the future.

### Positive interpretation
The lesson that Jera offers is that if we want to achieve great results, we cannot go against the natural order of things and that we need to go with the flow. Events and changes will come at the proper time and we must take note of opportunities for new beginnings. This Rune is concerned with reaping what you have sown and receiving

just rewards for your efforts, so it can indicate the end of a long project and a feeling of relief.

Jera can refer to intervention by a third party, such as when one engages the services of a professional person, and sometimes this indicates legal matters. It can also refer to buying a new home. Although the world may appear stagnant at the time of the reading and things will go more slowly than you would like, there will soon be movement in your affairs and you will soon be able to harvest the seeds you have planted. Things will happen in their own space and time. What you have put out into the world will come back to you. Jera often refers to the repayment of money and favors. Delays may sometimes occur with legal or financial issues because Jera acts as a reminder that these things take time. Jera promises a beneficial outcome that will come in its own time, so patience is essential. It warns against judging others harshly because you may soon be judged yourself.

### Negative or reversed interpretation

This Rune cannot be read in a reversed position, but in its negative form indicates that problems can be overcome with a little careful effort. It also indicates that legal help may be needed. You may have to pay for your past misdeeds or you may be following a path to which you are not suited.

### Magical uses

In magic, Jera is used to bring about change and also to bring your will into effect slowly and naturally. As an amulet it can be worn to make your inner vision into physical reality.

EIHWAZ

## Thirteen
### Eihwaz
*Eihwas, eoh, ei, ihwar, iwhaa, aihs, waer. The sound of*
*"e" as in "egg"*

**Origin**

This Rune means yew, which is a tree that is sacred to Runecraf and to the making of bows. The bow is associated with the hunting god, Ull. The yew is also taken to represent the World tree, Yggdrasil that Odin hung in until he obtained knowledge. The yew is said to contain the mystery of life and death, as its roots were thought to reach into the underworld.

Eihwaz is a Rune of wisdom and provides protection by helping to increase personal power and the ability to defend yourself. It is a powerful symbol of protection and also of banishing. Yew is both strong and flexible and these concepts are encompassed in Eihwaz. As the yew gives freely of its fruit, this Rune also represents patient and unselfish giving. However, the fruit of the yew is poisonous which strengthens its association with death. Eihwaz possesses the power of both death and regeneration and a re-growth from an old situation into the new.

Its position as the thirteenth Rune means that it is often considered as the death Rune, although, many scholars consider that the association of "unlucky 13" and Norse mythology is apocryphal. Prior to Christianity, thirteen was a lucky number, representing the thirteen lunar months of the year. The origin of unlucky 13 appears to come from Christian sources, being attached to the thirteen diners at the last supper and also in association with the sentencing of the Knights Templar on Friday 13th 1307. It may be that this event was where the "unlucky" association was first made and that it was only later connected to the last supper and other biblical sources. (Although Hindu culture pronounces 13 an unlucky number, in the west the association appears to have been relatively recent.) The yew tree is also associated with death in Christian culture by the fact that it is frequently planted in cemeteries, as it was believed it could trap the souls of the dead, also its roots reach into the realms of the dead and its branches into the realms of the living. Yew trees can live for centuries, so it may represent the of continuity of time.

### Positive interpretation

Eihwaz symbolizes strength, reliability, depend-ability and trustworthiness. It represents doing the right things and persevering until you have got them right. It is associated with the endurance and patience necessary to achieve the change in consciousness that allows for a spiritual rebirth. As a Rune of protection and of hunting, Eihwaz shows that you have your sights on a reasonable target and that you can achieve your goals. Although minor delays and obstacles are possible, they are unlikely to cause too much trouble. So long as you are flexible and able to work with change you can turn any situation to your advantage. Like the image of a bow being pulled back, this sometimes represents a time when you clear the decks and make ready for some new activity.

Often Eihwaz shows a tie to the past. When it appears in a reading, you may hear from someone from your past, and there is a possibility that things that were not previously dealt with previously can be successfully resolved now. It signifies a turning point in your life and as long as you can put up with temporary discomfort, it brings good results.

### Negative or reversed interpretation

Eihwaz cannot be read in a reversed position, but in its negative form it refers to the resurgence of an old problem that has not been properly dealt with. It also shows false nostalgia for the past and a sense of loss and confusion.

### Magical uses

In magic, Eihwaz is used to bring profound change and to overcome difficulties, especially when you are looking for a new avenue. As an amulet it can be worn to protect you from your own weaknesses by rendering you sensible and thoughtful.

PERTHO

# Fourteen
## Pertho
*Perth, perthro, perdhro, pretra, perthu, pairthra, pertra*
*perth, peorth. The sound of "p"*
### Origin

A variety of meanings have been associated with this Rune, ranging from dance, through fruit-tree to hearth. It is also associated with the magical powers of the earth, through an association with the Latin word "petra", meaning rock. Additionally it is associated with the vulva, so bearing an association with Freya, mother of the gods, as a symbol of female sexuality and sometimes of birth.

Its primary meaning is that of initiation, of things that are hidden and unexplained and of the working of the fates, which leads to its association with the Nornir. It points towards that which is beyond our powers. Powerful forces of change are indicated, so at times it represents surprises, gains or rewards that you did not anticipate. Being concerned with the deepest part of our being, Pertho refers to the bedrock on which our destiny is founded. It can refer to transition or letting go of everything. Those things that you know on an unconscious level can come into the light and help you to understand the higher meaning of things. Pertho suggests the vagaries of chance that cannot be controlled. It symbolizes the warrior who constantly tests himself against chance and luck. Because of this, it also represents luck in action or any gamble or risk that is undertaken. It represents the uncertainties of life and the interaction between your personal free will and the constraints of your circumstances.

Pertho is also the Rune of memory, recollection and of problem solving. It shows an unexpected resolution to difficult situations. As a Rune of mystery, it reveals hidden things and secret or occult abilities. Its appearance often refers to the disclosure of some sort of secret. In general terms, Pertho refers to mysteries, the occult, psychic abilities and revelation. Tradition says that if this is the first Rune to appear in a casting, the reading should be aborted because any advice that follows will change the course of fate and anger the Norns.

### Negative or reversed interpretation

In its negative form, Pertho may represent skeletons in the closet about to be revealed, and things from your past that you would prefer to keep hidden, coming back to haunt you. Pertho refers to disappointments and letdowns. An unpleasant surprise could be ahead of you and obstacles are likely to appear and confound all that you are trying to do. It is best to accept the passing of old patterns and concerns from your life. This is no time to take risks.

### Magical uses

In magic, Pertho is used to increase power and help gain wisdom. As an amulet, it can be worn as an aid in childbirth.

ALGIZ

## Fifteen
### *Algiz*
*Elhaz, algz, ezec, eolh, eloh. The sound of "z"*
### *Origin*

Algiz implies defense and protection, and has also been equated with the elk. It is a sign used to promote victory and protection as well as the strengthening of magical power and luck. It is often associated with the Valkyries as a protective force. It is also connected to the animal kingdom and our contact with animal forces. In ancient Scandinavian magic the "fear helmet" was considered a symbol of protection. This is made from four Algiz Runes engraved on four sides of the helmet and meeting in the middle, thus creating a helmet that symbolically protects people from their worst fears.

### *Positive interpretation*

As a Rune of protection, Algiz often tells of a fortunate new influence entering your life. It also suggests that this is the right time to follow your instincts. Friendships are in the forefront of your life now, and an old or new friend may offer assistance. It may tell of an opportunity that someone will offer you. Accepting the opportunity or offer can turn you in a beneficial new direction. It may indicate that a guardian angel is hovering in the background. Algiz indicates assistance and warning of danger, in addition to indicating those people and places that will give you support. It offers new opportunities and challenges, along with the emotional stability needed to cope with them. Things may be turbulent at this time but it indicates that you are making progress.

Algiz symbolizes resistant power and is the most powerful defense Rune. It acts as a shield that can repel evil. If you are sick, this Rune indicates the return of good health, and it can also signify friends and loved ones who help you to regain your health and strength. There is a slight warning for you to look after yourself and not to wear yourself out on behalf of others or to allow lame ducks to drain you.

### Negative or reversed interpretation

In its negative form Algiz describes vulnerability, danger and forbidden acts, because this is a time when you are vulnerable. It can suggest that you may have to sacrifice something for no perceptible gain. There could be someone you should avoid or perhaps an offer that you should refuse. Someone may be using you, although is possible that you are deceiving yourself or expecting something for nothing. It is advisable to be wary of new associations and also to avoid those who drain you or pull you down. Algiz can suggest a lack of contact with our survival instincts and a lack of communication with your true nature. It can also warn about a period of sickness or the continuation of poor health. The message here is to look after yourself first and only later to use your energies for the benefit of others.

### Magical uses

In magic, Algiz is used to give protection from negative impulses and to fill a place with power. As an amulet it can be worn for protection.

SOWELO

## Sixteen
## Sowelo
*Sol, sunna, sowelu, sowilu, sowilo, sigil, sowulo, sygil, sugil, sauil. The sound of "ss"*

### Origin

This is the sun Rune and it feminine in nature, as is the sun in Norse mythology and even in the modern German language. It is the counter force to Isa. Sowelu is often connected to the lightening bolt, to a flash of inspiration or to ecstasy. It strengthens spiritual and psychic powers and talents, and it provides enlightenment and success through individual will. It is a Rune of understanding, education and a transforming force that can represent high achievements, honor and obtaincd goals. Representing the sun as it does, Sowelo symbolizes that upon which all life depends. It is associated with the shining god, Baldur, the patron of innocence and light who is closely associated with the mistletoe, a shaft of which was set into blind Hodor's hand by Loki in order to kill Baldur.

### Positive interpretation

This Rune represents a higher form of joy, happiness and love. It is closely related to the heart and to the summer season. Sowelo symbolizes a strong positive force and life-giving warmth. Too little of it means lack of life and light, while too much sun brings drought and feeling of being burned out. Sowelo can resist death and disintegration and allow light to conquer dark. Its illumination allows you to see your goals more clearly. It promises good health, energy, clarity, optimism, confidence and understanding. It is a Rune of victory and success. It indicates a time when power is available to you for positive changes in your life. In matters of love, Sowelo is a wonderful Rune to find as it promises joy and happiness.

### Negative or reversed interpretation

Sowelo cannot be read in a reversed position, but in its negative form it indicates a sudden change, sweeping things out of way and possibly over-confidence or burn out. As a force, it can act as a weapon of destruction or it can clear away the old for the new. It can show your dark side - that side of your nature which is destructive to yourself and to others.

### Magical uses

In magic, Sowelo is used to gain energy, healing and strength. As an amulet it can be worn to increase vitality.

# Tyr's Aett

*Tiwaz, Berkano, Ehwaz, Mannaz, Laguz, Inguz, Othila, Dagaz.*

**TIWAZ**

**Seventeen**
*Tiwaz*
*Tyr, tir, tiwar, teiwas, teiws, tyz, tiwaz, tiw. The sound of "t" or "th" as in "then"*

### Origin

This is the Rune of Tyr, the god of war, giver of victory and protector from harm. Wolfsbane, or "Tyr's helm" was used on arrowheads as a poison and it was reputed to be a principal ingredient of witches' flying ointments. Tiwaz is also identified with the "Spear Rune" that an aging warrior supposedly cut into his own flesh so that he might enter Valhalla. It is commonly found on English cremation urns. Its meaning is primarily that of justice, as Tyr was the god that presided over the general assembly. Associated with the pole star, it represents guiding principles that are steadfast and that can be relied on when a traveler wishes to judge his position. In divination, it often refers to judgment, matters of law, decisions or guidance. As Tyr's attribute is the sword, he represents unselfish courage and the warrior's energy. His clarity and wisdom can cut through the deepest of darkness. Tiwaz brings the courage to enter dark realms, without knowing where or when you will come out into the light again. It gives an inner balance and it symbolizes potency.

### Positive interpretation

Tiwaz is a Rune of victory and success in any competition. It shows that you are ready to fight for what you believe in and it promises success in battle. It denotes strong motivation and great strength and will power. Tiwaz suggests the winning of disputes and the maintenance of law and order, therefore, it is a Rune of stability, organization and order. It indicates where your duties lie and it denotes self-sacrifice and responsibility. Dedication, bravery, objectivity and authority are symbolized by this Rune.

Tiwaz relates to binding oaths, and thus to commitment, and while this is often taken to mean committing yourself to a cause or a fight, it can also relate to marriage vows - although nowadays of course, this can mean a commitment that doesn't actually include vows taken in a Church or Register Office. Tiwaz is an extremely masculine Rune, so this suggests the kind of marriage where the husband has the kind of strong and determined nature that makes the marriage hot and exciting. On the one hand the sexual passions between the partners might run high, but with such a domineering man in charge, the woman will need to sacrifice some part of her own independence or identity. Battles might rage where two strong-minded people fight for supremacy, and jealousy and rage may never be far removed from the heat of sexual passion. Nevertheless, this is the kind of marriage that can stand the test of time and end up with two good friends entering old age together. In some castings, this can indicate a new romance, but if the reading is for a woman, she must weigh up whether she wants to spend her life loving an exciting and difficult man even before she gets into the situation.

### Negative or reversed interpretation

In its negative form, Teiwaz may represent cowardice, weakness and lack of initiative. It suggests defeatism, or perhaps conflict where there should be harmony. It may indicate a rigid nature of the kind that does not listen to others or to sense. It indicates failure in any context or competition, which may be due to giving up too easily when difficulties occur or as a result of acting in haste. If there is a question of romance, the man in the picture may not be honest, and he may also be selfish and irresponsible. Matters of trust and confidence are main issues but on some occasions this Rune can refer to a relationship composed of short-lived lust.

### Magical uses

In magic, Tiwaz is used to give strength, protection and victory. As an amulet it can be worn for protection.

BERKANO

**Eighteen**
*Berkano*
*Bjarka, Berkana, bairkana, bern, beorc, bjarkan,*
*bairkan. The sound of "b"*
*Origin*
Berkano means birch tree. This tree was regarded as sacred and it was associated with the fertility rites of springtime. Berkano is a feminine Rune, related to the earth goddess, so it represents manifestation and rebirth. In northern Europe it is representative of physical beauty and attraction. It is strongly associated with Frigga in her maternal, caring aspects and thus represents all types of attractive female qualities. It also symbolizes nourishment, healing powers and natural forces. Berkano is the Rune of the earth, which receives the sacrifice or seed and then holds it within itself, guarding and nourishing it until the time has come for it to return to the outside world again.
*Positive interpretation*
This Rune represents birth or rebirth and it is also often referred to as the "birth Rune". The birth in question might literally be the birth of a child, but it can also refer to the birth of an idea. Berkano is considered to be especially powerful in women's matters. It is concerned with the power of woman, with birth and with regeneration. It can be thought of as the family Rune, so it may refer to a happy family event. Being associated with motherhood, it can

relate to one's own mother, but it is especially connected to the ideas of fertility and the care and nurture of infants and children.

Berkano represents new ideas, fresh starts and a new projects - sometimes even a new romance, but whatever the new situation might be, it will be something that brings happiness.

New growth is also symbolized here; tenderness and compassion. The new idea or project will need careful tending if it is to grow and develop, because if it is not properly attended to - like a neglected child, it will die off. This Rune is strongly connected with the family and home. It is also a Rune of co-operation and perhaps a nicer and more peaceful atmosphere within a family. Berkano represents increased understanding and emotional stability. It hints at hidden transformation, awareness and growth that may be attained after asking for spiritual help and guidance.

### Negative or reversed interpretation

In its negative form Berkano may represent infertility, and it can also indicate sickness for yourself or for someone else around you who is sick and who needs to be cared for. It often indicates an unfortunate domestic situation, fraught with arguments, and in the worst cases it can indicate too much sacrifice or martyrdom. Sometimes secrecy within a marriage or elsewhere - along with carelessness or loss of control - are among the negative aspects of Berkano. If you are deeply unhappy, this Rune suggests that you ought to examine your own character in order to understand what is interfering with your own growth or what you are doing to draw such matters towards you. You may be putting your own desires above those of others or you may be putting up with unreasonable behavior. Although a negative Berkano can indicate success, it is possible that this success will not be long lasting. In matters of business, the ventures that are involved will have trouble getting started or they may fall through. Business plans may need to be put aside until a later date.

### Magical uses

In magic, Berkano is used to heighten fertility and help with women's problems. As an amulet it can be worn when wishing to make a fresh start.

**EHWAZ**

## Nineteen
### Ehwaz
*Eih, ehwo, eho, evz, egeis, aihws, ior, eow, eh. The sound of "e" as in "egg"*

**Origin**

Ehwaz is associated with the twin gods or heroes, and also the divine twins or two horses. Ehwaz represents the harmonious relationship between two forces. It is closely connected to the "fetch", which is the horse that carries you on your journey between the two worlds and with the eight-legged Sleipnir, the horse of Odin. Ehwaz facilitates soul's travels or the shaman's journey and it represents a journey in consciousness that is protected and guided. Horses have been regarded as sacred since the earliest times, and they were believed to privy the counsels of the gods. The horse was frequently regarded as sacred to Freyr.

Ehwaz is also a symbol of fertility.

***Positive interpretation***

Due to Ehwaz's association with rapid progress and physical movement. Thus, it represents all forms of communication and travel, and perhaps your communications equipment, your vehicle or your modes of transport. It can even be associated with hallucinogenic drugs or magic mushrooms that are used as a means of traveling between the two worlds. However, it is also associated with the natural changes that occur during life.

Due to its attachment to the ideas of movement and change, Ehwaz may indicate a change of occupation or a new address, although it often indicates a journey. You will soon be able to tackle problems in the right manner, which will bring a quick improvement and a new outlook on life. As long as your intentions are serious your projects should flow smoothly from beginning to end and have a successful outcome.

Ehwaz symbolizes instinct, progress, trust, loyalty and faith and it may indicate a partnership or marriage. It certainly signifies true friendship and fidelity.

*Negative or reversed interpretation*

In its negative form Ehwaz shows that not all possibilities are open to you and you may be better off avoiding action or looking for new opportunities. On one hand, a lack of real direction may be a problem, while on the other hand hasty actions and reckless behavior will cause accidents. If you need medicines or medicinal drugs at this time, take care with these in case you overdose yourself or use something that causes an adverse reaction. You may feel confined and restless and in need of a change, but it is best not to make decisions too quickly as it is too easy to waste time by taking the wrong direction. Problems may arise in connection with travel and transport, or it may be your ambitions that are being frustrated. Perhaps your loved ones are not in tune with your wishes and this may cause setbacks and frustrations. There may be health worries in connection with domestic animals or family pets.

*Magical uses*

In magic, Ehwaz is used to build power and bring people together or break them apart. As an amulet it may be worn to aid in communication.

MANNAZ

# Twenty
## *Mannaz*
*Manna, mannuz, mann, madr, madir, mannarz,*
*mannazold, madhr. The sound of "m"*
### Origin

Mannaz means man, either as an individual or as part of humankind, and it naturally also includes women. Mannaz is thought to offer powers for defense and protection. It is a Rune of human existence and of the natural events of life and death, which makes it the Rune of mortality. It also represents interdependence and support, in addition to duty and responsibility. When cast, it may indicate the activities or situation concerning an individual or a group, or it can also represent connections to others. It is a Rune of assistance that suggests a need for help or a willingness to give aid to others. This Rune represents our basic human qualities and our shared experience. It stands for the social order that supports the community and allows us to live in peace and to reach out and fulfill our potential. The qualities it emphasizes most strongly are those of being part of society, co-operation and support - along with happiness. Mannaz is associated with Heimdal, the god who was raised by humans, and it is considered to be a Rune of the mind rather than the emotions.

*Positive interpretation*

Mannaz contains two somewhat connected ideas, the first being your own status within your community or within your circle and the way that others perceive you and the second is that it shows where you can go to look for help from others. As regards the first of these concepts, you need to assess your attitude towards others and also theirs towards you and also to reflect on your own behavior before criticizing that of others. Thus this suggests a time for time for personal reflection, and it is a Rune of the rational mind, intelligence, structure, reason and consciousness.

Looking at the second Mannaz concept, this represents a group effort or some form of pulling together and it shows where you can expect to receive help or co-operation from others. The help you receive may be practical but it could equally come in the form of good advice. This can signify a good time for implementing plans and it speaks of constructive activity. It may show a new acquaintance who will enlarge your outlook and contacts. You must consider motives and behavior of others and consider the likely drawbacks to putting yourself under too much of an obligation to them. Nothing happens quickly when Mannaz turns up in a casting, so thought, consideration and analysis of the facts will be needed before taking action. After this it may be a case of waiting for the group to shape up and pull the project together.

*Negative or reversed interpretation*

In its negative form, Mannaz can indicate that a problem has been blown up out of all proportion, and it can also suggest that you are on the verge of giving up. At this point in time, you may need advice, but you will definitely need to maintain a positive attitude. The help you hoped for might not be forthcoming. You could be feeling isolated and lonely. In some cases, this may actually be self-inflicted situation that has arisen out of a need to retreat from the world and to reflect on your life. Your self-esteem will be low and you may lack the ability to communicate clearly with others. In some cases, there may be an enemy or an untrustworthy person around you. In yet other cases, it can tell of a domineering father or of male homo-sexuality.

*Magical uses*

In magic, Mannaz is used to help social relationships and represent a particular person or group of people. As an amulet it can be worn to assist with reflection.

LAGUZ

**Twenty-one**
*Laguz*
*Lagus, laaz, lagu, logr, lagurz. The sound of "l"*
**Origin**
Laguz means water. The Norsemen used the sea and rivers to move across continents and also for fishing, and so the sea and other bodies of water were considered a path to wealth and fertility. In addition, water was considered to be an expression of the unconscious and of the undiscovered mysteries of life and death. Like the water in a well, Laguz can bubble up from secret depths, but a lake can also reflect the view from above and therefore keep what is hidden under it a secret. Water seeks its own level and it takes the path of least resistance. Water is associated with death and the final journey. It holds all secrets and it represents the unknown. Laguz is associated with the Vanir god Njord, a wealthy deity who was associated with the sea. Seagulls and seals were sacred to him, as were fjords, safe harbors and inlets; his personal emblem is the seashell.

*Positive interpretation*
Laguz symbolizes your emotions and intuition, your tears and also your subconscious. It represents nudity, sensitivity, receptiveness and vulnerability. It represents your ability to float along in the river of life and to adapt to circumstances with sensitivity. You will need to go with the flow or be washed away. Although you cannot live

without water for long, you cannot live for long in it. Instinct and the depths of emotions are shown by this Rune. It shows your ability to empathize and to adapt to a situation. Your secret fears are revealed and encompassed in this Rune. It advises you to use your intuition, to be aware of and alert to your feelings, and to find ways of fulfilling your emotional needs. Flexibility and adaptability are necessary. It suggests that sometimes you need to simply experience life without evaluating or understanding it.

In practical terms, Laguz can refer to the pleasurable aspects of life, to good fortune and success in trading - especially international trade or goods that are carried over water. It may mean that you have to wait for another party to make their moves before you can proceed with business, but it does indicate that success will come along. When this happens, you need to get moving and make the best of the opportunities that are on offer. Laguz can also denote good relationships and happy marriage and a safe emotional haven. Even when a relationship is going through a difficult patch, it shows that it is basically a good one. Alternatively, if a relationship has ended, if you are lonely or sad, it suggests that someone nicer will soon come along.

### Negative or reversed interpretation

In its negative form Laguz tells of failure to draw on your instincts. You may be ignoring your inner voice, which warns against wrong actions or taking on things that are beyond your capabilities. Your fears may cause your emotions to be inhibited. You may suffer from depression or moods related to a desire to have something or someone who is not available to you, so a more flexible attitude will be needed. There is no point in cursing your fate or in drowning your sorrows in alcohol. This may be a time of confusion in your life where you take wrong decisions and misjudge things. There is a temptation to take the easy way out or to do something that is clearly wrong. There may be a woman in your life who will bring trouble.

### Magical uses

In magic, Laguz is used to stabilize the emotions and intellect and to help in confronting fears. As an amulet it can be worn to give strength and enhance your psychic abilities.

INGUZ

## Twenty-two
### Inguz
*Ing. The sound of "ng" as in "thing".*
*Origin*

Ing is the horse-god of fertility. Other symbols for this sign are the boar, the cuckoo, the apple and laurel trees. Ing is considered to be a doorway to the astral plane. In Germanic languages, "ing" can mean son of, as in "atheling" or son of the king, and it even turns up in science fiction books as earthling, meaning someone from earth as opposed to some other part of the galaxy. There is a possibility that Ing was an actual human who belonged to the nation known as the eastern Danes. This deity is certainly associated with Denmark, and by extension with Britain after much of it was taken over and run by the Danes and unified under King Canute (King Knut).

The Norse god of fertility, Freya, is associated with this Rune. It can be a Rune of horses, although Freya preferred to ride a wild boar named Gullinbursti (golden bristles), and the bristles on the animal's back were said to symbolize golden wheat.

*Positive interpretation*

Inguz is associated with the start of a new season or phase, the beginning of a new project and of fertility and growth. It indicates health and well-being and also a fertile mind that is full of good ideas, in addition to the energy and motivation to make a start on a new project.

Sometimes, it is necessary to see off an old project before making a fresh start, so Inguz can indicate that loose ends need to be tied up, jobs completed and the decks cleared in readiness for the next phase. Even if there is no indication of a new phase at this point in time, Inguz tells you that it is just around the corner, so it is well to clear the way for it.

Sometimes this literally means clearing out cupboards, the loft or clearing barns, offices or even the car in readiness for something new. Sometimes this can indicate inheritance, and probably having to clear out somebody else's house and perhaps to keep some part of its contents for yourself. In other circumstances, this indicates a time to get rid of those people who pull you down, make use of you for their own ends or who may hinder your progress or your ability to make a fresh start. Inguz can suggest that you take a break or a holiday in order to step back from your situation and allow you to take a different perspective.

### Negative or reversed interpretation

This Rune cannot be read in a reversed position, but if surrounded by negative Runes, it warns that fear, indecision or laziness may cause you to miss opportunities. It also suggests that you consider whether the words and behavior of others designed to hold you back or to keep you from making necessary changes. It may suit their interests for you to remain stuck in a situation that is not doing you much good. Whatever the situation, courage and faith in the protection of your spiritual guides will help you to break free and to make the fresh start that you need.

OTHILA

**Twenty-three**
*Othila*
*Othala, othilia, odal, othal, ethel, odhal, utal. The*
*sound of "o" as in "old"*
**Origin**
Othila means inheritance in the sense of anything of value that can be handed down or passed on and this includes knowledge. It encompasses the customs and attitudes of the ancestors as well as the inheritance of property, material things or physical attributes. It represents the wise management of family assets. It also represents loyalty, duty and the responsibilities that go along with maintaining family ties.

Othila is associated with land, so it represents cultivation in all its aspects. This may imply actual crops or some form of creativity through culture, art and craftsmanship. It can represent the growth of the intellect and emotions. Othila is concerned with establishing and making your mark on history. It is also representative of your ancestors and of any previous lifetimes that you may have experienced. Othila is often associated with Odin, the father of the gods. It resists arbitrary rules and seeks to preserve individual and collective liberty within the framework of natural law. Like a family secret, it is something to be carefully guarded and watched over.

*Positive interpretation*

Othila refers to possessions, land, the home and those items that you already own or those that you will acquire, which means that it can also relate to inheritance. However, it is just as likely to tell of inherited talent, behavior or characteristics. This Rune may refer to religious, group or family traditions that have become hallowed and which are comforting, especially in times of stress. Othila refers to family history, group loyalty and to your roots. It can relate to patriotism, love of your country, an interest in history (either history in general or family history), a religious group or the clan, tribe or dynasty to which you belong. It can mean becoming part of a group of like-minded people that makes you feel safe and useful. Othila can indicate help from older people or old friends. It symbolizes the values of your family and culture.

It may indicate that you are living in a closed world and that you need to open up more, or that you are too tied to the family, the clan or the past. Thus it suggests freedom and independence through releasing ideas and even releasing yourself from those things that keep you stuck.

*Negative or reversed interpretation*

In its negative form, Othila indicates that you may be bound by old conditioning and refusing to let go of outmoded ideas and concepts. Sometimes this denotes overturning the established order of things and bringing chaos to the family or group. Perhaps you need to consider what benefits you and others. It can refer to a lack of roots or of isolation. Sometimes it indicates delay and frustration. It can indicate disputes over money, goods and inheritance and legal problems related to land and property; so where this is concerned, it is important to be patient and pay attention to detail. It can warn against trickery or theft. In modern terms, a negative Othila can refer to problems with vehicles or machinery. You may lose some of your possessions, possibly due to trying to move too fast. Success is possible but this is further away than you would like it to be.

### Magical uses

In magic, Othila represents land, property and ownership. As an amulet it can be worn to bring wisdom and power to you from all sources.

DAGAZ

**Twenty-four**
*Dagaz*
*Daeg, dags, daz. The sound of "d"*
**Origin**

Dagaz means day. This contained a period of both dark and light as the Norse counted their days from evening to evening with the midpoint being dawn. Sometimes it relates to the hours of daylight, and specifically to noon. It is often associated with Thor, the god of lightning who brings inspiration, so it represents transformation and awakening, and the passage from darkness to light. Dagaz can represent paradox and the balancing of opposites as complements rather than as contradictions. Dagaz is a Rune of clear vision and enlightenment and it represents time and space. It is the Rune of polarization and of good fortune. The coming of daylight offers security and a time when you can see your foes coming and so counteract them. Fears and phobias can also be countered at this time.

**Positive interpretation**

Dagaz is a wonderful Rune to find if your life has been in limbo or if you have not been making progress, as it suggests that a time of waiting will soon be over and that major events and turning points are on the way. It is a Rune of good fortune. Dagaz refers to a time when work can successfully go ahead. As one of the Runes that is identical when reversed, its independence is further enhanced, because no matter how life turns out, its energy cannot be turned or reversed and its transformation is always positive. Dagaz may signify protection when new people or situations enter your life. Dagaz has great protective powers and is a Rune of health, prosperity and new openings. It can prevent harm and encourage helpful energies. It is a Rune of change, of gradual but slow improvement, prosperity and completion. It represents the end of an era and the beginning of a new day. Occasionally, Dagaz can bring secrets out into the open or it can show why a particular route or activity has been blocked or closed to you. This revelation allows you to move forward in the kind of clear vision that you have when the sun is shining rather than continuing to grope about in the dark.

Sometimes Dagaz is associated with children and it indicates that any children in your circle will be happy and successful. It can also indicate fun and happiness, new and pleasurable activities and a burst of fresh energy.

### Negative or reversed interpretation

As a Rune of increase and growth Dagaz has no negative aspects, so even when surrounded by difficult Runes it shows an inner strength that can be used in times of difficulty. It counteracts delay and shows slow and steady progress. It brings the end of an era and the dawning of a new day full of hope and optimism. It can indicate a major change for the better. At worst, it can show that you are drawing problems to yourself by dwelling on them too much.

### Magical uses

In magic, Dagaz can be used to invoked an awakening of the senses. As an amulet it can be used for protection and it is often used for the protection of entrances.

BLANK

## Wyrd - the Blank Rune

Modern sets of Runes usually include a blank Rune but this is not traditional; many Rune readers prefer not to use it - after all, the Runes are letters of the alphabet and there is no such thing as a non-existent letter. However, for those who do wish to include this Rune, it is associated with Wyrd which is not a god as such, but a kind of collective energy that controlled the activities of the Norns who themselves controlled the fates. In some traditions, Wyrd is said to be the mother of the Norns and the one who wove the web of fate that covered the then known world. Therefore, Wyrd can be viewed as the force that judges both gods and mortals and that rewards or punishes them for their actions. It can also be considered to be the Rune that cuts short their mortality.

### *Interpretation*

In terms of a reading the blank Rune of Wyrd means fate, destiny, kismet or karma and thus, circumstances and events that are beyond our control. Those of us who live in the modern, western world find it hard to believe in fate or karma, and we prefer to think that own free will can override destiny. However, accidents happen, people can suddenly become bereaved, New Yorkers discovered a particularly cruel form of fate on September 11, 2001. On the other hand, there are people who win a fortune on a lottery or find themselves inheriting money and goods from relatives who they did not even know existed or who they knew about but did not expect anything from. Life is not all in our hands - a lot is, but sometimes it is just a matter of destiny, and all we can do is live through both good and evil times and learn from them.

# Attitude and Ritual

### A Professional Attitude

At this point in time, you may be considering becoming a professional consultant. You may only wish to give readings for charity, or you may simply want to be a competent amateur. Whatever your motivation, treat yourself to a copy of "Prophecy for Profit" by Sasha Fenton, as this contains everything you could wish to know about the "business" side of this kind of work. This book is useful for any kind of small business enterprise, but it is specifically aimed at those who want to give readings as a part or full-time career. Even if you do not intend to make a living as a consultant, this book will show you how to go about things, and how to prevent your "hobby" from costing you unnecessary money or aggravation.

When someone asks a professional consultant for a reading they expect to find that the consultant is skilled, competent and knowledgeable. The average client thinks that the consultant has a special gift or skill and the client just knows that this is not something that anybody can do. Even though we know that learning the Runes is relatively straightforward, this is not what people want to hear. A member of the general public likes to have something of a show put on for them as part of their reading so it is important to create the right atmosphere. This does not mean that you have to dress up like Gypsy Rose Lee or make your surroundings look like a New Age shop, but there are a few simple things that you can do. If you can use a separate room for your readings, you may be able to hang wallpaper, curtains or pictures that have a mildly spiritual appearance. If you do not have a separate room or you do not want to make your room look special in this way, at least ensure that your surroundings are clean and tidy, and that the place looks inviting. Enhance the area with cut flowers or a pot plant or two (if you are into Feng Shui, you will prefer living plants to cut flowers). Some consultants like to play quiet music in the background, some like a low light that gives an intimate atmosphere. Some like a lighted candle in the room and some burn incense or use one of those aromatherapy oil burners. It is a matter of personal taste. Take care with incense though, because too much of it is cloying and it can actually make some people cough. Take care with candles and burners - do not set the place on fire!

If a person is desperate for a reading, they will not care where or in what kind of surroundings this occurs, but generally speaking, a client will be happier in a nice place than in unpleasant or makeshift surroundings. They will take the reading more seriously and they will be happier to pay up at the end of it. Although a reading can be conducted anywhere, it is best if you and your questioner are comfortable and unlikely to be disturbed. Sitting opposite each other can create a feeling of distance between you and your client, so you may feel more comfortable sitting side by side. On the other hand, you may prefer to have plenty of space to lay out your Runes. The important thing is to find a comfortable position for all concerned.

Before you even begin, you need to be in the correct state of mind. You need to put your client at ease and convince him or her that you are reliable and trustworthy. You need to speak about the Runes with confidence and authority. Before taking any clients you should be able to recognize, name and describe the meanings of Runes without referring to books. While you are still learning, you should give readings for friends and family to improve your skills and to bring yourself up to standard. You should only start professional work when you are quite ready for it. Once you feel that you are competent to be let loose on the public, and better still, after you have worked in the professional field for a while, why not consider approaching, for example, the British Astrological and Psychic Society to be vetted as a BAPS Consultant? After vetting, you will be issued with a Certificate of Competence, which is renewed annually (as long as you don't blot your copy book in some damaging manner). A formal qualification will give you the confidence that you have reached an appropriate standard and it will also help to put the minds of your clients at ease.

When doing a reading for someone else, you need to remember that this is their reading and should be addressing their needs. Projecting an air of confidence will encourage your client to have faith in your abilities. The more a clients trust you the more likely they are to listen to and act upon any advice received from the Runes.

*Money Matters*

There is nothing wrong with accepting payment for your work. Interpretation of the Runes is a skill requiring study and practice, and just like anyone else providing a service you are entitled to payment. It is best to set a rate for the job when making the initial appointment. Once again, Sasha Fenton's book will tell you all you need to know about this side of things.

### Ethics

If you become a BAPS Consultant, you will be required to sign a Code of Ethics before your Certificate of Competence will be issued to you. This will concentrate your mind on the right and wrong ways of going about your work.

It can sometimes be difficult to present the information you read to a client. Advice offered by the Runes can be frank and may not always be what the client wishes to hear. Although there is nothing wrong with offering your interpretation as diplomatically as you can, you also need to guard against sugaring the pill so much that the original meaning becomes lost.

Even if you are only doing a reading for practice you should still take your reading seriously and think carefully about the way you word your information. Some people may claim to disbelieve in the Runes but what you say will still have an effect on them. The best thing is to imagine how you would feel in their position. It is all too easy to inflict emotional damage, and you will not want your clients to leave feeling worse than when they arrived!

Rune reading is tiring and draining. It is not a good idea to undertake a reading when you are feeling less than your best. People can be demanding, and some thoughtless types will ask you to give them a reading no matter how bad you feel or how late the hour. Few matters are so urgent that they cannot wait a short time. When someone is in distress it can be very difficult to stand back from them, but it may be necessary for the preservation of your own mental health. What you are aiming to do is to offer information, reassurance and grounds for hope, but if a client is in desperate straits and you are not a trained and skilled counselor, there is a limit to what you can do. In this case, it would be worth having the names of a couple of trustworthy counselors to whom you can refer such a client or even suggest that they contact the Social Services, a lawyer, an accountant or in extreme circumstances, the Samaritans.

Tolerance is essential for any reader. You may have completely different views to your client on any number of matters, but the reading is for them and it is their views that matter. You also owe your client complete confidentiality. If you want to discuss your reading with another practitioner, then you should not only seek permission from your client, but also make sure that their identity is not revealed.

### Rituals

Although any surface can be used for your Runes, many people prefer to have a special cloth. Some people like to have separate cloths for each spread, with the spreads marked out on them. Additionally, many Rune-casters like to put symbols of the different elements on the table with them. A candle may be used for fire, a saucer of water for water, a feather for air and a stone for earth. These can be purely decorative or used in your reading by passing the Runes over each in turn before laying them out. Earth is usually placed to the north, air to the east, fire to the south and water to the west.

Before you begin a reading you should wash you hands. Not only will this help to protect you Runes but it will also show respect to them. Your washing can be turned into a ritual act of purification. While washing away the dirt on your hands you can visualize your fears and doubts being washed away.

Some Rune-casters like to speak as part of their ritual before beginning the reading. It is not necessary to use poetic language or invoke any gods if you do not believe in them. If you are asking your Spiritual Guide or god to help you do a true and correct reading then that is all that you need say. Saying something simply for effect is likely to backfire on you. If your client detects that you do not believe in what you say then you will have lost all credibility before your reading even starts. Whether you hold a belief in the deities of Norse mythology or not, it is important to remember that others do, and you need to treat their beliefs with respect. At the least you should have and acknowledge an awareness of the complex mythology underlying the Runes.

# Casting the Runes

### How Best to Use the Runes

Runes can be used for an "overview" reading, but frankly, they are not designed for this, because their main purpose is to focus on a specific question and to answer it. That is fine if the questioner understands this, but it can be a problem when dealing with a member of the general public.

When a client visits a professional consultant, it is unlikely that he/she will be willing to tell the consultant exactly what the problem is. Indeed, if the consultant were to ask the client what he/she wants to know, the client will invariably wave a hand in the air, look around the room and give a vague, "Oh, just tell me what you see," kind of answer. After all, the client is paying for the reading, so why tell this supposedly all-seeing, all-knowing, professional clairvoyant anything? Once the consultant has gained the client's trust, only then can the consultant focus on the particular worry that forced the client to make the appointment in the first place. Therefore, it may be better to use some other kind of divination in the opening stages of a reading and reserve the Runes for later when you know that you can pose a specific question for the Runes to answer.

When using Runes, it is best to decide on a question and to make this concise and specific. The questioner needs to be clear about the question, about who is involved in it and perhaps also the time frame in which it is set. You cannot expect the Runes to give a helpful answer if the questioner is not honest about the true nature of the question.

### A significator Rune

If you are throwing the Runes, rather than laying them out in a spread, you need to select a Rune that appears to embody the question to stand as the significator of the question. Do not pull the Rune out of the bag, leave all the Runes in place but jot the Rune's name down or make a mental note of it. Thus, if the question refers to a matter of business or money, choose a Rune that represents this, or if it the questioner wishes to know about a health matter, select an appropriate Rune. If the significator Rune shows up in the reading, things are unlikely to change. The significator is chosen by looking at the heart of the question and deciding which of the Aettir it belongs to. A question about love, life and happiness belongs to Freya's Aett. If the question concerns intellect, understanding and spiritual growth it belongs to Hagal's Aett if it a question about daily life, work, house moves, family problems and so forth, it belongs to Tir's Aett.

### Reversed Runes

There are sixteen Runes that can be reversed and it is a matter of debate whether reversed Runes have any special meaning, especially as there is no evidence to show whether reversed Runes were or were not treated differently by the ancients. It is an over simplification to consider reversed Runes as negative, because some, like Hagalaz, cannot be reversed and are not very nice to see in a reading whether they are upright or reversed. Each Rune has both positive and negative within it, so it may be better to regard a reversed Rune as a warning to the client to take the right kind of action or to side step a forthcoming problem.

*NB:* Some Tarot readers see a reversed card as indicating an event that has already passed, others see it as an event that has not yet come into being - so perhaps this technique might prove useful for the Runes as well.

*Positioning*

It is natural to want to read each Rune in isolation, but by diving in and doing it this way, you are likely to miss out on a whole level of information. The Runes in a spread interact with each other. Two Runes together in a spread can react in a variety of different ways as follows:

Their meanings may be entirely separate and they may not react with each other at all, but this can indicate that two separate issues are plaguing the questioner at the same time.

They can have separate meanings, but the second Rune reinforces or clarifies the meaning of the first. It may add more information about the topic or it could represent a person involved in the situation described by the first Rune.

The two Runes may have very similar meanings, which emphasizes the importance of the message within the reading as a whole.

*Modifiers*

Some Runes are considered to act as "power" Runes, dominating those around them and modifying the tone of surrounding Runes. Those that relate to gods or start one of the Aettir demand such attention. These are Fehu, Ansuz, Thurisaz , Hagalaz, Tiwaz  and Mannaz.

The presence of one or more of these Runes in a spread shows that the gods are taking a particular interest in the situation. Wunjo can also moderate the tone of surrounding Runes, and while it cannot change the meaning of any Runes nearby, it may reduce some of the problems indicated by other Runes.

### Throwing the Runes

The simplest method is to pour the Runes onto the floor and then interpret each Rune that lands facing upwards. If a Rune falls onto its back or rests on its side, you should ignore it. If a Rune falls on its side between two Runes that connect in a meaningful way then that Rune can be interpreted in its basic meaning. When choosing the Runes to read in this way you need to look over your cast carefully to decide which Runes are closest to each other.

Often a defined area is used to throw the Runes into. Create this by using a casting cloth of a size that depends upon the size of your Runes. Two circles, one inside the other should be drawn on the cloth. The inner circle represents the past, the outer circle the present and the area outside both circles represents the future. Alternatively, the central Runes may represent the heart of the question, while those further out might represent environmental or other factors.

Another method is to point the top of your cloth towards the north and then to consider any Runes that fall in this direction to represent some kind of difficulty, while those that fall towards the south can be seen as useful and helpful - even if they are difficult in nature. Runes that fall to the east represent things that are known, or events arising out of the past, while those that fall to the west indicate events that have yet to be revealed. When you consider the geography of northern lands, the north is a hard place, the south is where the light and warmth come from, the east was the land that was known and the west was an unknown quantity.

If you decide to read the Runes out of doors, you could use a piece of chalk or a stick to draw a circle on the ground. Stand in the circle and focus on the question, gently throwing the Runes and taking note of where they land. The closer they are to you, the more significant they are to the question. You also take note of how close they fall to the person who is asking the question, to the other Runes and to the circle itself.

When you have fixed the question in your mind and thrown your Runes, you can begin by allowing your intuition to take over in a similar way that those who divine by tea leaves, coffee grounds, sand or stones do. Look for any patterns in the way the Runes fall. If the shape reminds you of something then allow this to guide you. For example, if the pattern reminds you of a boat or an airplane, a journey could be indicated. If the pattern reminds you of a the shape of a specific Rune symbol, that particular Rune will be relevant to your question - even if it isn't included in pattern itself. Start by reading the Runes that are nearest to you and then continue by working outward - away from yourself.

If you sit at a table and toss three Runes onto the cloth, note where the Runes fall and note the symbol on each of the Runes. If you wish to use reversed meanings, ensure that you turn the Runes over from left to right or right to left, moving them horizontally rather than vertically, so that you will not reverse an upright Rune, or vice versa.

### Basic information on spreads

You are almost spoilt for choice when it comes to finding suitable spreads for Rune reading, and your choice of spreads is very much a matter of personal preference. You may find a particular spread that you feel comfortable with and stick to that one, or you may wish to use a variety of spreads with each one being chosen to suit the nature of the question.

It is probably best to begin with something simple, because it can be confusing for a beginner to try and deal with too many Runes at once. As you gain more experience you can use more complex spreads that will provide more information. Before making your decision about which spread to use, you must consider the Questioner and his/her requirements, the issue in question and how you feel in yourself at the time of the reading. If you do not feel like laying out a host of Runes and you consider that a simple spread will offer sufficient information, it is unnecessary to use anything more complex.

In no time at all, you will discover those spreads that feel natural to you and you will probably end up using them on a regular basis. However, you may occasionally use others - even if they feel artificial to you, and there will be some that you truly dislike and never use. You may well decide to settle on just using a three-Rune spread, but whatever you end up doing, it is worth trying as many spreads as possible at this stage so that you can discover which of them suit you best.

Here are some points that are worth bearing in mind:

The number of Runes that you use in a spread determines the amount and nature of the information given.

With a higher number of Runes you may experience difficulties in drawing together the information and providing a sensible summary.

Using more Runes means spending a longer time on the reading and doing more work. This may be an advantage or a disadvantage depending upon the circumstances.

When your questioner has a decision to make, a spread of one to three Runes is ideal. A larger number of Runes is useful when a fuller picture is needed, but then the position of each Rune in the spread will also need to be considered.

Each Rune has many potential meanings, not all of which will be appropriate to the question at hand and each Rune can perform one or more of the following functions:

| Function | Rune action |
|----------|-------------|
| Descriptive | Describing a situation. |
| Advisory | Commenting on a situation and offering guidance. |
| Predictive | Suggesting how events may turn out in the future provided the rest of the reading is heeded. |
| Representative | Representing a person, animal, object or problem. |

The more Runes you use in a spread, the more functions they will need to serve. In a single Rune spread, the Rune has to describe the situation, offer guidance and give an idea of the outcome. If you use seven Runes in a reading, each Rune may fulfill a single function, although its position in a spread can narrow the options for meanings.

*Casting Runes onto a cloth on a table*

In cool, wet countries like Britain, the chances are that you will be casting your Runes indoors and on a table - at least on some occasions.

If you prefer to draw a specific number of Runes for a reading that will be used in a specific layout rather than simply thrown, concentrate on the question and draw the number of Runes that you wish to use and then throw them lightly onto your cloth. After noting the initial appearance of the cast, go on to read each individual Rune. If you wish to use the Runes that are face down turn them over at this stage. You need to look for the combination of meanings and the relationships that the Runes have with each other in terms of their distance from each other or whether they overlay each other in addition to reading each individual Rune.

The Runes that fall in the center of your cloth represent the predominant issues of the question. Those that are away from the center can be considered outside the main issue. See how many Runes land face down, as these can show hidden elements that are behind the scenes. The more Runes that land upright, the more positive the reading. Runes that are touching or covering other Runes are closely working together in some way.

Remember that you can also use the north, south, east and west method, you can consider the central Runes to represent the past and the outer Runes increasingly pointing the way to the future or you can see the inner Runes as the heart of the matter and the outer ones as surrounding circumstances. The choice is yours but you will probably soon find the method that you feel most comfortable with.

# Simple Spreads

### A Single Rune Spread

Drawing a single Rune is the simplest possible method. It does not enable you to look at a situation in detail but it can provide a quick answer or it can help you or your questioner to make a decision. Clear your mind and think of your question and then pull one Rune from your bag. Consult the meaning of this Rune and see how it applies to the question and to the question. If you wish to use this for yourself, you can take one Rune every morning to give you a guide as to what sort of day to expect.

One Rune can be used in this way to answer a specific "yes or no" type of question. In this case, if the Rune falls in the upright position - the answer is yes. Runes that cannot be reversed should always be considered to be upright.

### Three-Rune Spreads

Spreads that use three Runes are extremely popular. They are easy to use and they offer a reasonable amount of information. There are many different three-Rune spreads, and here are several ideas for you to try for a layout consisting of three Runes laid in a row:

Position one:     The likely outcome of a situation.
Position two:     The action that is required.
Position three:   The current situation.

Position one:     The past.
Position two:     The present.
Position three:   The future.

Position one:     The problem or issue at hand.
Position two:     The best course of action.
Position three:   The likely outcome if the action that has
                  been advised is taken.

Position one:     Questioner's present physical condition.
Position two:     Questioner's present mental condition.
Position three:   Questioner's present spiritual condition.

You can try laying two Runes side by side, with a third placed below the second.

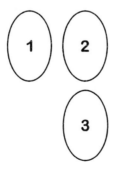

The first position describes the current situation, the second the factors affecting the situation and the third gives advice. This spread has no predictive element and is best for those who want to think about their present situation or to make a decision based on current circumstances.

With just three Runes, there are a variety of possibilities that can influence the outcome of the reading. In the first of the following three ideas, the first shape puts the Runes at an equal distance apart, suggesting that each Rune is of equal value in the reading. The second is like an "L" shape and has an association with learning. The third resembles an arrow and thus illustrates a direction that the questioner should take.

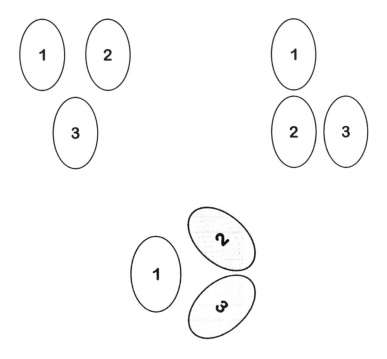

*Four Runes - The Four Dwarves Spread*
The spread is followed by two methods for reading it.

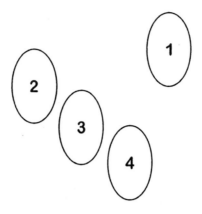

*Reading one*
 1.  Past desires in relation to the question.
 2.  Present desires and how the questioner feels
     about the question.
 3.  The desires and feelings of others and how they
     affect the question.
 4.  The questioner's heart's desire that he or she
     keeps hidden from the world.

*Reading two*
 1.  The basic influences that surround the question.
 2.  Problems and obstacles that may affect the
     outcome of the question.
 3.  Positive influences at work with regard to the
     question.
 4.  The immediate outcome.

*Five Runes - The Cross of Thor Spread*
This spread has two Runes performing a predictive function, and is therefore good for a reading where matters of money, business or income are paramount.

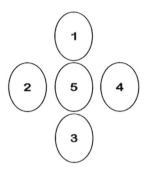

*Interpreting the Cross of Thor*
1. The situation.
2. The obstacles.
3. Supportive forces.
4. The short-term outcome.
5. The long-term outcome.

*The Five Elements Spread*
The layout is the same as the previous spread, but the order in which the Runes are read is different. This spread is intended to give an insight into the personality, behavior or feelings rather than events.

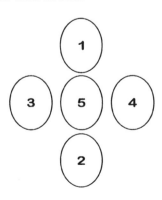

1. The intellect position. Studies, invention, composition, science and the arts.
2. The desire position. Battles, lust, anger, cruelty, hatred, desire and destruction.
3. The strength position. Labor, endurance, persistence, silence, suffering and woe.
4. The love position. Family, friendships, devotion, obsessions and fantasy.
5. The balance position. The questioner, also politics, religion and magic.

The following are further readings that you can use for a five-rune layout of this type:

*Reading one*
1. The physical body, surroundings and environment.
2 The questioner's present state of mind.
3 The creative forces at work.
4. The questioner's emotions in regard to the question.
5 The spiritual influences.

*Reading two*
1. This shows where you currently find yourself in life.
2. This shows what is on your mind.
3. This shows what is in your heart, your deepest desire.
4. This shows your primary intentions.
5. This shows your future actions and deeds.

The following still uses the familiar cross layout, but with the Runes placed in a different order.

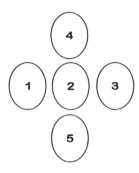

Here are two interpretations that can be used with this layout.

### Reading one

1. Rune one suggests that something from the past that caused the current situation.
2. Rune two describes the current situation.
3. Rune three shows the outcome.
4. Rune four shows what help the questioner can expect.
5. Rune five shows the obstacles before her, also those aspects of a situation that cannot be changed and must be accepted.

### Reading two

1. The overview - the current situation.
2. The challenge - problems you are facing.
3. The action - what is needed to fix the problem.
4. The sacrifice - what the questioner needs to let go of.
5. The new overview - the developing situation.

*The Six Rune Spread - and one extra?*

This spread is based on the Celtic Cross spread used for Tarot cards.

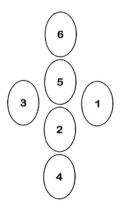

1. The past - what lies behind the situation.
2. The self - where the questioner currently is.
3. The future - what lies ahead of the questioner.
4. The foundation.
5. The challenges the questioner will face.
6. The new situation.

A seventh Rune may also be drawn at the end of the reading to help tie the others together. This is the Rune of resolution.

*The Runic Cross Spread*

The following layout can be used in two different ways.

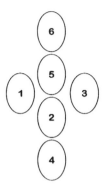

*Reading one*

1. The past
2. The present state of mind.
3. The possible future.
4. The basic influences underlying the question.
5. Events and factors that will help or hinder a successful outcome.
6. The most likely outcome.

*Reading two*

This is particularly useful for a questioner who wants to know about his or her career, and it is sometimes called the Career Mirror.

1. The questioner's current position.
2. The challenge being faced by him.
3. The questioner's position of greatest strength and ability.
4. The questioner's past perception with regard to the matter at hand.
5. The questioner's future perception.
6. The future outcome.

*A Seven Rune spread - The Seven Worlds Spread*

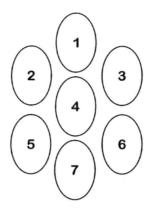

*The reading*

1. That which is right or what is required of the questioner by fate.
2. Things working in the questioner's favor: also expansion, growth, fertility and pleasure.
3. Force and strength, though a difficult Rune can suggest weakness.
4. The core of the question, the questioner himself.
5. The questioner's skill, purpose and ability.
6. Dangers and forces opposing the questioner, also the effects of greed, anger and fear.
7. Hidden factors and things that are not as they seem.

# Complex Spreads

*Seven Rune Spread - The Combined Runes Spread*

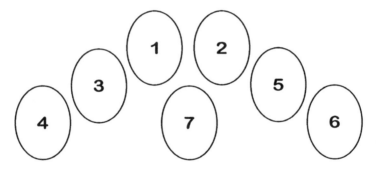

This spread involves reading the Runes in pairs.

The first and second Runes describe the issue or problem.
The third and fourth Runes show factors of the past that
exert an influence on the current situation.
The fifth and sixth Runes represent the advice the Runes
are offering.
The seventh Rune is the outcome of the situation if the
questioner follows the advice that is given.

*Seven Rune Spread - The Mimir's Head Spread*
The Runes in this spread are read in pairs.

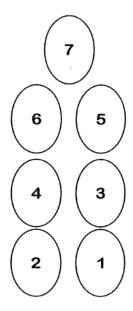

Positions 1 and 2 signify the issue at hand.
Positions 3 and 4 represent the reasons for the problem.
Positions 5 and 6 represent solutions and ways of
    resolution.
Position 7 represents the result and final outcome.

*Eight Rune spreads - Mimir's Head Two*

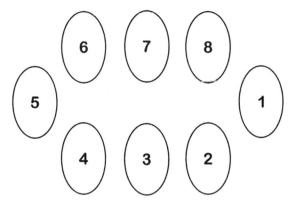

This eight Rune spread represents the wheel of the year, reflecting its quarter and cross quarter divisions. Each of the spokes is ruled by a Rune. The meaning of each Rune that is drawn is determined in relation to - or in combination with - the Rune that governs that particular spoke or "house". If a Rune falls into a house that is ruled by itself, then its meaning is doubled, while if it falls into a house whose Rune means the opposite, both are neutralized. When you interpret this reading start with the house that corresponds with your question, moving in an anticlockwise direction around the wheel until all of the Runes are read.

| Position | Interpretation |
| --- | --- |
| 1. The House of Berkano | Birth, motherhood, beginnings, fecundity, the mother goddess. |
| 2. The House of Laguz | Growth, flow, increase in energy, second sight, initiation. |
| 3. The House of Dagaz | Possible sudden changes, polarities, the balance between day and night, "dawn Rune" of entry. |
| 4. The House of Thurisaz | Protection from enemies and personal attack, defensive and resistant powers. |
| 5. The House of Kanauz | Learning, creativity, artistic mastery, inspiration, illumination. |
| 6. The House of Hagalaz | Transformation, evolution within a fixed framework, metamorphosis. |
| 7. The House of Jera | The Rune of the yearly harvest, reward, completion, success, luck. |
| 8. The House of Algiz | Inner strength, defense against all harmful forces, the Rune of divine guidance and assistance. |

*The Nine Rune spread - The Grid of Nine Spread*

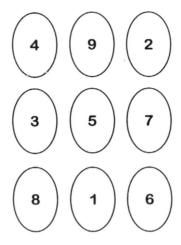

This ancient symbol is also known as the Magic Square of Saturn. All of the lines add up to fifteen and the square gives a total of 45. This is an appropriate spread for questions dealing with protection from negativity and personal attack, injury, bad luck or evildoers.

**The bottom row represents the past.**
Position eight shows influences from the past, position one shows the basic past influences and position six shows the questioner's attitude to those past events.

**The middle row represents the present.**
Position three shows the hidden influences that are operating at the time of the reading, position five stands for the current state of affairs and position seven shows the questioner's attitude towards the present influences.

**The top row represents the future.**

Position four shows the hidden obstacles, delays and
problems that can affect a successful outcome,
position nine shows the best possible outcome,
and position two shows the questioner's response
to the outcome.

*Ten Rune Spreads - The Tree of Life Spread*

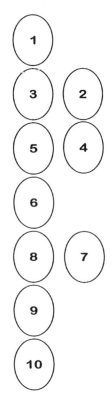

This spread is designed to give a concise overview of the questioner's life. The positions represent the roots, trunk, branches and top of the Tree of Life.

One    This symbolizes the questioner's highest ideals and standards of excellence.

Two and three  The second Rune represents the questioner's current energy level, while the third, represents his/her physical and mental experiences. Read these two Runes as a pair.

Four and five  The fourth Rune signifies the questioner's ethical virtues and personal moral code while the fifth shows the area of his/her most recent victories and successes. Read these two Runes individually and then as a pair.

Six     The sixth Rune represents the questioner's health and issues related to health.

Seven and eight The seventh Rune denotes personal issues of love and trust, while the eighth Rune stands for creativity in the arts, crafts and procreation. Read these two Runes combined as a pair.

Nine    The ninth Rune points to the questioner's powers of imagination and creative ideas.

Ten     The lowest Rune sits at the roots of the tree and represents the questioner's living conditions and the state of his domestic situation.

## *Eleven Rune Spread - The Cosmic Axis Spread*

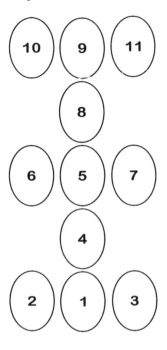

1.   This reflects the major past influences that bear upon the questioner.
2.   This denotes the unconscious response to this major past influence.
3.   This signifies the conscious response to this major past influence.
4.   The lower link position represents the results of the influences that have led to the present state of affairs.
5.   This position denotes the present.
6.   This suggests current unconscious responses.
7.   This shows current conscious responses.
8.   This reveals the results of the present influences if the questioner does nothing to alter the flow of energies.

9.      This signifies the major outcome of the question at hand.

10.     This refers to the unconscious response to the outcome.

11.     This represents the conscious response to the outcome.

### *Eleven Rune Spread - The Four Quarters Spread*

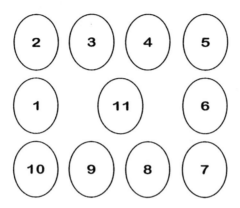

This spread is based on the four quarters of the year, and it is used when you need a precise answer to a complex question, in addition to an overall view of life for the past six months and the coming six months

Positions one, two and ten represent the first quarter and show the questioner's present state of mind.

Positions five, six and seven represent the second quarter and show helpful or opposing influences in regard to the question.

Positions three and four represent the third quarter and reveal what will happen if things continue in their current direction.

Positions eight and nine represent the possible outcome of the question six months from now.

Position eleven represents the overall tone of the spread.

*Twelve Rune spread - The Celtic Knight Cross Spread*

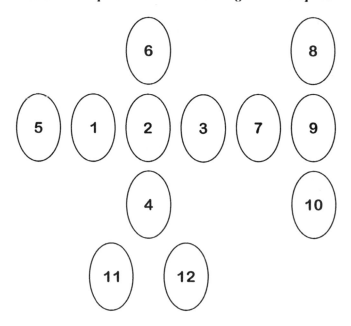

This spread is adapted from the Celtic Cross Tarot spread and it is used in much the same way. The Celtic Knight's Cross allows the Rune-caster to focus deeply on the particular problem that the questioner wishes to inquire into. For instance, the questioner may be interested to hear about his/her career, personal relationships, health, finances, buying or selling a house or anything that is going on in the immediate environment. Once the questioner has some idea of what the options are and what is likely to change or remain the same, then he/she can make sensible decisions.

It is a good idea to select a Rune to act as a significator of the questioner. After choosing and finding the Runes, place the selected Rune in position one. The remaining Runes can then be put back into their bag, shaken around and then drawn and laid one by one in the remaining eleven positions.

First: this is the Significator Rune that represents the person for whom the reading is being done.

The second position signifies the question.

The third position denotes immediate future influences, positive and negative.

The fourth position reflects childhood and other past influences.

The fifth, the position to the left, reveals present influences just about to move out of the questioner's life.

The sixth position at the top of the cross shows possible influences in the future, depending upon the polarities of the positions next to it.

The seventh position represents future influences that will impact the question at hand.

The eight and nine positions signify the questioner's hopes and fears.

The tenth position shows influences from the questioner's family and friends that are both positive and negative.

Eleven and twelve are final-outcome positions. Two Runes appear in this final position in order to give the questioner a couple of options or a wider outcome reading. These two Runes can be read in combination with each other.

### Thirteen Rune spreads - The Runic Wheel Spread

Twelve Runes are laid in a circle with the first Rune taking the place of where the number nine would be on a clock. The next Rune is placed where the 8 o'clock position would be, and so on in a counter-clockwise direction around the wheel. The thirteenth Rune is laid in the center of the circle. The Runes are placed so that their narrower sides face the center. When interpreting each Rune you need to pay attention to those on either side of it.

### *The Futhark Spread*

This spread uses all the Runes and it is designed to give an outline of the year ahead. Each of the Runes is read in relation to the Rune that rules its position. Note that there are three rows of eight - or three Aettir. Also note that each position is posed as a question that relates to the Rune that rules the placement. Naturally, it is the Rune that lands up in each position that provides the answers.

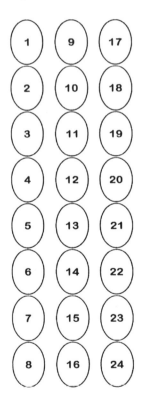

1. Fehu -       What will provide the questioner with
                money and prosperity?
2. Uruz -       What will give the questioner inner
                strength and good physical health?
3. Thurisaz -   What will defend or destroy the
                questioner?
4. Ansuz -      What will inspire the questioner and
                drive the questioner's intellect?
5. Raido -      Where will the questioner travel to?
6. Kenauz -     What will the questioner create and come
                to know?
7. Gebo -       What gifts will be given to questioner?
8. Wunjo -      What will bring the questioner joy,
                pleasure and happiness?
9. Hagalaz -    What will transform and change the
                questioner?
10. Nauthiz -   What will the questioner need?
11. Isa -       What will inspire the questioner and
                drive the questioner's intellect?
12. Jera -      What harvest will the questioner reap?
13. Eihwaz -    What choices and challenges lie ahead?
14. Pertho -    What hidden talents and abilities will
                come into being?
15. Algiz -     What life and death issues will come up
                in the next year?
16. Sowelo -    What will be the questioner's guiding
                light?
17. Tiwaz -     What will be the state of the questioner's
                legal affairs?
18. Berkano     What will create growth and beauty?
19. Ehwaz -     What partnerships and relationships will
                the questioner form over the next year?
20. Mannaz -    What will the questioner's social life be
                like?

21. Laguz -     How will the questioner feel
                (emotionally), over the next year?
22. Inguz -     What form will the questioner's sexual
                expression take?
23. Othila      What property or knowledge will the
                questioner inherit/receive in the next
                year?
24. Dagaz       Where will the questioner find balance in
                his/her life?

# Rune Magic

The primary use of Runes is for divination, which means as an oracle that offers information on the past, present and future, and also to advise, warn and guide. The information received can be used to help an individual make a decision, especially once the questioner understands the possible consequences of that decision. In divination, as in magic, it is the human will that brings success and this can be helped by a consultant who understands the beliefs inherent in the system, coupled with confidence in his or her skills. However, in addition to Runes being used for divination, they may also be used for magic. Rune magic is a separate field of study, so what follows is a very brief overview, so if this is where your interest lies you may wish to study the subject further. To achieve any success in Rune magic you need to develop a deep understanding and familiarity with literary sources, such as the Havamal as well as with the Runes themselves.

There is a story of an ancient Rune-master being called to the bedside of a woman who was sick. He found that someone had carved Runes in the belief that they would make the woman fall in love with him, but the Runes were badly chosen and they caused her to become sick. The moral of this story is that using the Runes badly can cause more harm than good.

In the ancient Northern magic tradition there were essentially two different strands of magical practice. Seidhr, which was shamanistic in nature, involving trances, dreams and astral travel to and through the nine worlds. Like many ancient forms of magic, this could have a darker side that is intended to bring sickness and even death. Galdr, which was closer in nature to ceremonial magic. It involved the use of talismans and charms, particularly those spoken aloud and most Rune magic is of this sort.

### The Eights

There are eight different techniques that are involved in Rune magic. The number eight has great significance with respect to the Runes as reflected by the three Aets.

The first stage is selecting the right material to be used for magical Runes.

The second technique relates to cutting or marking of the Rune glyphs. Making a Rune was a precise process that involved cutting into the material to be used, and the cuts had to be in a made in a specific order if the Runes were to be used for magic. When Runes are made for this purpose, the Rune-caster needs to be aware of the meaning of the Runes and sure that what is being cut is appropriate.

Thirdly, the cut Runes are then stained; there are a number of references about staining the Runes with blood if they are to be used for magic. Modern Rune readers suggest that this is purely symbolic and that red paint should be used instead.

The fourth stage is that of testing, and this means not only evaluating the Rune to be used but also a testing of the Rune-caster himself.

The fifth stage is that of evoking or asking. This is a spoken command that transforms the glyphs from carved characters to activated Runes.

The sixth stage is the stage of blessing the Runes, performing a ritual to dedicate them to a specific god and preparing them for use.

The seventh stage is of sending. This technique focuses the magical power of the Runes and sends it towards the target of the spell.

Finally, during the eighth stage, the Rune-caster feeds the Rune with strength and energy. This may also refer to deactivating unwanted charms.

*Names as Charms*

The use of individual Runes as charms is well established in both the archaeology and in the literature of Northern Europe. The magical meaning of the Runes is closely related to their divinatory meanings – for example Fehu is used magically to attract wealth, although it could also be used negatively to deprive another of material comfort. Positive magic with Runes is known as "weal working" whereas negative magic is known as "woe working". Both the positive and negative forms of magic were used in the past. However, the majority of charms were defensive and protective. For example, instead of trying to kill an enemy a charm would be used to make sure that his attacks had no effect. There are several references to charms being activated with spoken commands that were said to trigger them. The exact Runes used for charms as described in the Havamal magical text is open to debate.

*Bind Runes*

Bind Runes are those that are combined to increase their magical power. Two or more Runes are imposed onto each other to from a new pattern, and this is then used as a personal symbol or worn as a pendant. There are two main types of bind Rune, those made from a persons name or initials and those made from specific Runes to combine their qualities.

It is quite popular to construct a Rune out of those that make up the initials of your own name, but these may not actually be Runes you may want to be closely associated with. The second method involves combining Runes according to the result that you are looking for. For example, if you need courage and strength combined with resilience and good judgment, you would combine the Runes Uruz and Tiwaz. Wearing this as a pendant would enable you to draw these properties into your being.

When making a Bind Rune, the two that are chosen for the purpose need to be combined in a way that is pleasing to the eye and that has a kind of symmetry. Choosing suitable Runes for the effect you require takes serious thought, but that is only the first stage. If you choose the wrong Runes you will still have a result, but it may not be the one you had hoped for. Another way in which Rune magic may be worked is to carve a suitable Rune three times on a talisman or candle, as this is held to represent completion on all three planes. Traditionally, the magical energies are classified into three parts, which are the elements, the Runes and the gods. In combining the Runes each of these is addressed. Other symbols besides Runes were used in Old Norse magic. Some of these were variations on the Runes and others simply referred to a single concept or deity, such as the hammer of Thor.

To make a talisman you need to carve or paint the Rune onto an item and carry it accompanied by a suitable herb or crystal.

Finally, July 15 is the Feast of Rowana, the patron of the secret knowledge of the Runes.

## MAGICAL CORRESPONDENCES - Table 1

| The Rune | The God | The Color | The Stone | The Tree |
|---|---|---|---|---|
| Fehu | Aesir | Light red | Moss agate | Elder |
| Uruz | Vanir | Dark green | Carbuncle | Birch |
| Thurisaz | Thor | Bright red | Sapphire | Hawthorn |
| Ansuz | Odin | Dark blue | Emerald | Ash |
| Raido | Foresti | Bright red | Chrysoprase | Oak |
| Kaunaz | Freya/Dwarves | Light red | Bloodstone | Pine |
| Gebo | Odin/Freya | Deep blue | Opal | Elm |
| Wunjo | Freyr/Elves | Yellow | Diamond | Ash |
| Hagalaz | Ymir | Light blue | Onyx | Yew |
| Nauthiz | Normir/Etins | Black | Lapis lazuli | Rowan |
| Isa | Rime/Thursur | Black | Cat's eye | Alder |
| Jera | Freyr | Light blue | Carnelian | Oak |
| Eihwaz | Idhunna/Ullr | Dark blue | Topaz | Yew |
| Pertho | Normir | Black | Aquamarine | Aspen |
| Algiz | Valkyrjur | Gold | Amethyst | Yew |
| Sowelo | Sol | White/silver | Ruby | Juniper |
| Tiwaz | Tyr/Mani | Bright red | Coral | Oak |
| Berkano | Frigg/Nerthus/Hel | Dark green | Moonstone | Birch |
| Ehwaz | Freya/Freyr Aclis | White | Iceland spar | Holly |
| Mannaz | Heimdal/Odin | Deep red | Garnet | Ash |
| Laguz | Nhord/Baldr | Deep green | Pearl | Willow |
| Inguz | Ing/Freyr | Yellow | Amber | Apple |
| Othila | Odin/Thor | Deep yellow | Ruby | Hawthorn |
| Dagaz | Odin/Ostara | Light blue | Crysolite | Spruce |

## MAGICAL CORRESPONDENCES - Table 2

| The Rune | The Flower | The Herb | Astrology | The Tarot |
|---|---|---|---|---|
| Fehu | Lily of the valley | Nettle | Aries | The Tower |
| Uruz | Nasturtium | Sphagnum moss | Taurus | High Priestess |
| Thurisaz | Honesty | Houseleek | Mars | The Emperor |
| Ansuz | Morning glory | Fly agaric | Venus | Death |
| Raido | Snapdragon | Mugwort | Sagittarius | The Hierophant |
| Kaunaz | Gorse flower | Cowslip | Venus | The Chariot |
| Gebo | Wormwood | Heartsease | Pisces | The Lovers |
| Wunjo | Larkspur | Flax | Leo | Strength |
| Hagalaz | Fern | Lily of the valley | Aquarius | The World |
| Nauthiz | Crocus | Bistort | Capricorn | The Devil |
| Isa | Sweet pea | Henbane | The Moon | The Hermit |
| Jera | Cornflower | Rosemary | The Sun | The Fool |
| Eihwaz | Lilac | Mandrake | Scorpio | The Hanged Man |
| Pertho | Chrysanthemum | Aconite | Saturn | Wheel of Fortune |
| Algiz | Sedge | Angelica | Cancer | The Moon |
| Sowelo | St. John's wort | Mistletoe | The Sun | The Sun |
| Tiwaz | Red hot poker | Sage | Libra | Justice |
| Berkano | Moonflower | Lady's mantle | Virgo | The Empress |
| Algiz | Forsythia | Ragwort | Gemini | The Lovers |
| Mannaz | Foxglove | Madder | Jupiter | The Magician |
| Laguz | Water lily | Leek | The Moon | The Star |
| Inguz | Gentian | Selfheal | New Moon | Judgment |
| Othila | Snowdrop | Clover | Full Moon | The Moon |
| Dagaz | Pot marigold | Clary | Half Moon | Temperance |

# Initials

If you fancy using your initial as a talisman or engraved on something and threaded through a leather cord as a pendant, the following table will show the corresponding Rune and letter. However, take care that your initial suits your requirements and that it is not a difficult or unlucky Rune. If your initials are SS you may decide against this, while if your name begins with an H, you will conjure up the destructive power of Hagalaz or an I or EE as in a name like Eve or Yvonne, you will be drawing the frozen and immobile power of Isa.

| English | Rune | Comments |
|---------|--------|------------|
| A | Ansuz | |
| B | Berkano | |
| C | Kaunaz | |
| D | Dagaz | |
| E | Ehwaz | as in ever |
| E | Isa | as in eel |
| E | Eihwaz | as in hay |
| F | Fehu | |
| G | Gebo | |
| H | Hagalaz | |
| I | Isa | |
| J | Jera | |

| | | |
|---|---|---|
| K | Kaunaz | |
| L | Laguz | |
| M | Mannaz | |
| N | Nauthiz | |
| O | Othila | |
| P | Pertho | |
| Q | Kaunaz | |
| R | Raido | |
| S | Sowelo | |
| T | Tiwaz | |
| U | Uruz | |
| V | Fehu | Stands for V |
| W | Uruz | |
| X | Algiz | |
| Y | Isa or Jera | |
| Z | Algiz | |
| Ng | Inguz | |
| Th | Thurisaz | As in thing |

# Runic Calendar and Clock

You may like to check out the calendar to see which Runes rule the various weeks of the year. Each Rune rules a fortnight, so in this way you can check out the Rune for your date of birth or for any date in any year. For example, if you have something special planned for a particular day or week or perhaps a fortnight's holiday, you may like to see what the Runes have to say about this. In addition, each hour of the day is ruled by a Rune, so if you have a special time planned for some event or for a meeting, see what the Runes have to tell you.

It is interesting to note that Hagalaz coves Halloween - and some say that the name Halloween derives from a form of the word Hagal or Hagalaz.

## Table of Dates and Hours

| Dates | Runes | Hours |
|---|---|---|
| 29 June to 14 July | Fehu | 12:30 to 13:30 |
| 14 to 29 July | Uruz | 13:30 to 14:30 |
| 29 July to 14 August | Thurisaz | 14:30 to 15:30 |
| 14 to 29 August | Ansuz | 15:30 to 16:30 |
| 29 August to 13 September | Raido | 16:30 to 17:30 |
| 13 to 28 September | Kaunaz | 17:30 to 18:30 |
| 28 September to 13 October | Gebo | 18:30 to 19:30 |
| 13 to 28 October | Wunjo | 19:30 to 20:30 |
| 28 October to 13 November | Hagalaz | 20:30 to 21:30 |
| 13 to 28 November | Nauthiz | 21:30 to 22:30 |
| 28 November to 13 December | Isa | 22:30 to 23:30 |
| 13 to 28 December | Jera | 23:30 to 00:30 |
| 28 December to 13 January | Eihwaz | 00:30 to 01:30 |
| 13 to 28 January | Pertho | 01:30 to 02:30 |
| 28 January to 12 February | Algiz | 02:30 to 03:30 |
| 12 to 27 February | Sowelo | 03:30 to 04:30 |
| 27 February to 14 March | Tiwaz | 04:30 to 05:30 |
| 14 to 30 March | Berkano | 05:30 to 06:30 |
| 30 March to 14 April | Ehwaz | 06:30 to 07:30 |
| 14 to 29 April | Mannaz | 07:30 to 08:30 |
| 29 April to 14 May | Laguz | 08:30 to 09:30 |
| 14 to 29 May | Inguz | 09:30 to 10:30 |
| 29 May to 14 June | Othila | 10:30 to 11:30 |
| 14 to 29 June | Dagaz | 11:30 to 12:30 |

# Index

# S

# Prophecy for Profit

*"The Essential Career & Business Guide for those who give Readings"*

## Sasha Fenton & Jan Budkowski

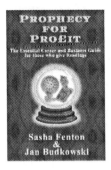

The right price for consultations... Startup costs...
The equipment you need... Building up your clientele...
Finances & cashflow... Organisational methods...
Your spiritual pathway... Psychic protection...
Stress and the self-employed... The Media...
The Marine Bandsman Syndrome... A mental & physical health guide...

and teaching & lecturing...

~~~~

Internationally recognized Astrologer, Tarot Reader, Palmist, Psychic and Author with sales of over 6 million books; who else but Sasha could produce a guide like this one?
Together with her husband Jan Budkowski, who adds over thirty years of financial and banking expertise, their combination delivers the most authoritative - yet easily readable - work of this nature that any consultant could ask for.

~~~~

*If you're serious about your career, you need this book!*


*ISBN 0-9533478-1-8*      *£10.95*
*240 pages*

# Modern Palmistry
*"A Unique Guide to Hand Analysis"*
Sasha Fenton

This is a comprehensive manual, useful for beginners and experienced palmists alike. It covers every aspect of hand reading, for the purposes of prediction, character reading, love, money and health.

In-depth coverage includes the way that past traumas are reflected on our hands, as they do in our psyches and even our spiritual pathway.

Sasha's well-known writing style makes easy work of complicated theories, while Malcolm is an artist as well as a palmist, so this book is packed with beautifully explicit and accurate illustrations.

~~~~

*"... an eminently practical work which deserves a place on the reference shelf of any potential palmist".*
Prediction Magazine, March 2004

*ISBN 1-903065-23-2*          *£10.99*
*208 pages*      *220 B&W illustrations*

# Fortune Telling by Tarot Cards
## *"A Beginner's Guide to Understanding the Tarot"*
### Sasha Fenton

Sasha brings over a quarter of a century of experience with the Tarot into this comprehensive Teach-Yourself Tarot book, taking the subject all the way through from a beginner's standpoint to a professional level.
Added to the usual Tarot book material, this new, revised edition of Sasha's 500,000 copy top-selling guide contains valuable information and considerations arising from Tarot students' questions - in particular, how to overcome the problem of linking apparently conflicting cards to make a lucid, synthesized reading.

~~~~

Contents include:-
Interpreting the cards - why readings don't always work - spreads & their uses - how to link cards easily - what happened after the guinea-pig readings in the previous edition!

~~~~

Striking new Tarot card illustrations throughout, designed by the acknowledged historian and astrologer, Jonathan Dee!

*ISBN 1-903065-18-6*          *£9.99*
*208 pages*

# Reading the Runes

We are pleased to advise that BAPS (The British
Astrological and Psychic Society) and Zambezi Publishing
came together to develop this project as the standard text
for their Rune Reading course.
If you are interested in studying for a recognized
qualification in Rune Reading, then you may wish to
contact BAPS for further details. Their address details are
given below.

~~~~

*Other courses available from BAPS, some of which are
already accompanied by Zambezi Publishing text books:
Psychic perception ~ Astrology ~ Classical Astrology ~
Karmic Astrology ~ Tarot ~ Palmistry ~ Chinese Oracles &
Feng Shui ~ Crystal Divination ~ Dream Interpretation ~
Graphology ~
Numerology ~ Practical Witchcraft & Magic ~ Introduction
to Alternative Health.
(Course list may change from time to time - contact BAPS
for latest details).*

~~~~

*Please address enquiries to:*
Dept Z
British Astrological and Psychic Society
P.O. Box 5344
MILTON KEYNES MK6 2WG

~~~~

Tel: +44 (0)906 470 0827
web: www.baps.ws    email: info@baps.ws

## Other selected titles from
# ZAMBEZI PUBLISHING LTD

**Tarot Mysteries** - *Jonathan Dee*
Why do the cards mean what they do? What link is
there between the Tarot and the Qabalah? Every
card is fully explained, with detailed historical
connections.
ISBN: 1-903065-24-0                    £10.99

**I Ching Decision Maker** - *Kim Farnell*
For beginners, with some advanced techniques.
Structured in the original approach to solving
dilemmas.
ISBN: 1-903065-32-1                    £8.99

**The Last Bastion** - *Ralph Harvey*
Highly respected book by the UK's leading authority
on the history and experience of traditional
witchcraft in England through the ages. Includes
Gardnerianism and other modern developments.
ISBN: 1-903065-40-2                    £14.99

**Practical Spellcraft** - *Leanna Greenaway*
A real witch's safe, gentle candle spells for all
purposes.
ISBN: 1-903065-22-4                    £10.99

**Fortune Telling with Playing Cards** - *Jonathan Dee*
The old, fun art explained, with astro-connections.
ISBN: 1-903065-31-3                    £9.99

**Develop your ESP** - *Nina Ashby*
No waffle, all practical techniques, covering auras
as well. Accompanying CD available.
ISBN: 1-903065-30-5                    £8.99

**Astrology for Success** - *Cass & Janie Jackson*
Covers aptitudes, careers, health & love. Maximise
your understanding of these vital life issues.
ISBN: 1-903065-28-3                    £8.99

*Full details of all our titles are available on
the Zambezi website at: www.zampub.com*

# ZAMBEZI PUBLISHING LTD
*"Much more than just books..."*

All our books are available from good bookshops throughout the UK; many are available in the USA, sometimes under different titles and ISBNs used by our USA co-publisher, Sterling Publishing Co, Inc.

*Please note:-*
Nowadays, no bookshop can hope to carry in stock more than a fraction of the books produced each year (over 130,000 new titles were released in the Uk last year!). However, most UK bookshops can order and supply our titles within a matter of days. If they say not, that's incorrect.
Alternatively, you can find all our books on www.amazon.co.uk, and many on amazon.com.
~~~~
If you still have any difficulty in sourcing one of our titles, then check our website or contact us at:-
Zambezi Publishing Ltd
P.O. Box 221, Plymouth
Devon PL2 2EQ
UK
Tel: +44 (0)1752 367 300   Fax: +44 (0)1752 350 453
web: www.zampub.com       email: info@zampub.com

*(Want to join our mail list, and be advised of new titles, or special offers from time to time?*
*We do NOT share your name with anyone else, and our list is infrequent - just email us your details, specifying snailmail or email preference).*

Printed in the United Kingdom
by Lightning Source UK Ltd.
104175UKS00001B/79-513